CATULLUS

CATULLUS

CATULLUS

Translation
by
Ewan Whyte

mosaic press

National Library of Canada
Cataloguing in Publication

Catullus, Gaius Valerius
    Catullus : bilingual Latin/English edition / translated by
Ewan White.

Includes index.
Text in English and Latin.
ISBN 0-88962-810-6

    1. Catullus, Gaius Valerius—Translations into English.
2. Elegiac poetry, Latin—Translations into English. I. Whyte,
Ewan, 1969- II. Title.

PA6276.E5W44 2004   874'.01   C2004-902574-0

Published by Mosaic Press, offices and warehouse at 1252 Speers Road, Units 1 and 2, Oakville, Ontario, L6L 5N9, Canada and Mosaic Press, PMB 145, 4500 Witmer Industrial Estates, Niagara Falls, NY, 14305-1386, U.S.A.

Mosaic Press acknowledges the assistance of the Canada Council and the Department of Canadian Heritage, Government of Canada for their support of our publishing programme.

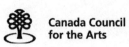

**Canada Council Conseil des Arts
for the Arts   du Canada**

Mosaic Press Canada:
1252 Speers Road, Units 1 & 2,
Oakville, Ontario
L6L 5N9
Phone/Fax: 905-825-2130
info@mosaic-press.com

www.mosaic-press.com

Mosaic Press U.S.A.:
4500 Witmer Industrial Estates
PMB 145, Niagara Falls, NY
14305-1386
Phone/Fax: 1-800-387-8992
info@mosaic-press.com

For my son Marcus

The translator wishes to acknowledge -
Darrick Wiebe, Catherine Moore, Sue Caderette, Rakel
Stephanian, Ricardo Sternberg, Patrick Georges Frank
Barbera, Raza Rizvi, Marie-Christine Trembley, Sean
Lipsett, Mike Kirney, Steven Myres, Brian Gunning,
Konrad Kozolowsky, Kelley Baker, Michael Dufton,
Terrence Smith, Merrill Shapiro, Keith Daniel, Howard
Aster, Robyn Rucchin-King, Jeff Herrle and the
Dooneys café guys.

INTRODUCTION

THE ROMAN POET CATULLUS wrote with a sensibility so close to our own that sometimes it is hard to believe he was an ancient writer. He did not write about legendary wars, the Roman Empire, or its founding myths. He wrote mostly about people he knew and either loved or hated. He drew upon a tradition that was originally Greek and he transformed that older tradition into something modern and graceful.

The poetry of Catullus, although celebrated in antiquity, only became known to a reading audience when it was was rediscovered in 1300. It was referred to later by Benevenuto Campesani in his elegiac verses as being found, "sub modio," "under a bushel." This sounds like a reference to Matthew 5:15, "Neither do men light a candle, and put it under a bushel, but on a candlestick; and it giveth light unto all that are in the house." Given the content of Catullus' book, a biblical comparison seems utterly hilarious to us.

How it survived the dark ages is a mystery. With other writers, we were not so lucky; of Catullus' contemporaries very little has survived. Just two short poems from the poet Furius, three lines from Gaius Cinna's epic poem *Zmyrna*, of Catullus' friend, and from the poet Calvus, not a single line has survived. This is unfortunate as Calvus's reputation was significant both as an orator and poet. Of the 'Zmyrna', Catullus wrote that people for ages would grow old admiring it, while a rival poet's work would meet its end as fish wrapping by a river. The survival of Catullus' book is, therefore, a gift. It might be greedy to ask for more!

Very little is known about the life of Catullus. The dates of his birth and death are uncertain. It is also unclear if he was a Roman citizen. He was probably born in 84 BCE and although his death was given by St. Jerome as 57 BCE, some of his poems seem to refer to later events, including Julius Caesar's first invasion of Britain in 55 BCE. Catullus was born into a wealthy family in the Roman province of Cisalpine Gaul, which was not yet part of the Roman State. Its inhabitants would only be granted Roman citizenship in 49 BCE, several years after Catullus' death. It is assumed that Catullus' father, who had considerable wealth, and had entertained Julius Caesar in his house in Verona, was a Roman citizen. Suetonius wrote a no longer extent 'life of Catullus'. The slim biographical information we do have is based upon what Catullus mentions about himself in his poetry; although it is unclear how much was for poetic effect.

Since the Renaissance, it has been argued that certain passages in Catullus' poetry did not warrant translation into English. The original Latin was reserved for dirty-minded students and scholars. Catullus never lacked readers. Poets from Ben Johnson to Irving Layton have written imitations of his work. This poem by Walter Savage Landor portrays the spirit of Catullus wonderfully:

> Tell me not what too well I know
> About the bard of Sirmio.
> Yes, in Thalia's son
> Such stains there are - as when a Grace
> Sprinkles another's laughing face
> With nectar, and runs on.

Even Horace Gregory's remarkable 1931 translation smoothes over many passages, losing some of the original humour. His translations are, as he clearly states, approximations in English. They are very far from traditional translations. Gregory successfully marries imitation with translation.

Elegant and rude, coarse and refined, Catullus' poetry is completely unlike the popular image of the work of a classical poet. Catullus' verse seems immediate and personal. His poetry was never part of the curriculum in Roman schools as were Horace's and Virgil's. Yet their poetry is not nearly as accessible as Catullus' and often requires a considerable knowledge of Roman mythology and history to enjoy it fully. With the exception of a few poems, Catullus's poetry can be read by anyone in any age. For example:

> Ipsitilla my sweet
> and luscious tart
> ask me to come by at noon.
> If you give me this
> give me one thing more.
> Leave your door unlocked.
> Please don't step out,
> but prepare for us
> a nine course feast of love.

> He is half crippled with arthritis
> and can hardly get hard enough to service her.
> She is made sick by the putrid odour from his armpits.
> You can consider yourself avenged my friend.
> In bed at night while he is stinking, and in pain,
> she must miss you; and more joy,
> they say he has inherited all of your diseases.

Catullus tried to obscure her identity by calling her Lesbia. The metrical matching of a pseudonym for a lover's name became a tradition in Roman poetry after Catullus' time. He may have been the first to use it in Latin. The names, Lesbia and Clodia, match metrically. She would only have to read her name in place of the name on the page. Lesbia was probably also chosen because Clodia was supposed to be a poet herself and the comparison to Lesbia would be a compliment to her high poetic standards. Sappho of Lesbos was one of the nine great lyric poets of ancient Greece.

In the very short poem '60' written about Lesbia, when reading down the first letters of each line, then reading up from the last letters of each line, you discover the hidden message: "natu ceu aes", 'in birth like bronze'. The words make us think of the fabulous warriors of the Bronze Age and we can imagine with little difficulty Achilles slaying some unlucky Trojan with 'the pitiless bronze.' This is a rather strong image and can be taken as a parody of itself, as when Catullus describes the death of Lesbia's sparrow in poem '3' as something that the Goddess Venus should be weeping about. In poem '60', the poet's anguish seems much more serious, although if he were that sick, it is remarkable that he would have had the wits to put in such an inventive acrostic. Many little surprises, like this, have been found in Catullus, some relatively recently.

> Num te leaena montibus Libystinis
> aut Scylla latrans infima inguinim parte
> tam mente dura procreauit ac taetra,
> ut supplicis uocem in nouissimo casu
> contemptam haberes, a nimis fero corde?

In English, without the acrostics:

> A lioness from the mountains of Libya
> must have given you birth or the great monster
> Scylla whose voice is the howling of dogs
> For how else can your cruelty be accounted for,
> I am dying, your contempt knows no bounds, you
> have no ear for my words and your heart is turned away.

Catullus tells us that his book was not popular in Rome. That is understandable; it was too new. Cicero read his poems, and Catullus' friend, the poet Calvus, had a correspondence with Cicero that filled two volumes, but it is now lost. We do not know what Cicero thought of Catullus and his literary circle but there was one poem addressed to him from Catullus. It seems it was just the type of poem Cicero would have liked:

> The highest praise of the sons of Romulus
> who have come before, and those yet to come,
> is yours for eloquence Marcus Tullius.
> Catullus, worst of poets, offers you his gratitude.
> The worst of poets as you are the greatest of Orators.

Catullus uses the word "disertisseme" (skillfully expressed), which is an epithet Cicero uses often in his writings and Orations. It is difficult to determine how this poem was meant to be received. Is this poem a compliment or is it poking fun at Cicero? There has been disagreement about this poem for a long time. I think Catullus is tugging lightly on Cicero's beard. It is difficult to imagine Catullus letting an opportunity for humour pass silently. Cicero would have had to interpret it for himself. Perhaps it refers to a running joke between them?

There are two longer poems in the book of Catullus. Poem '61' is an epithalamion or marriage poem for a wealthy Roman patron. Poem '64' is a longer poem in a genre the nineteenth century nicknamed Epyllion or little epic. As this poem is the only one of its kind to have survived it is difficult to assess. Its construction is deliberately artificial, although the speeches of Ariadne and Aegeus seem consciously to go beyond the descriptions of the woven landscape on the coverlet. With its many beautiful lines and descriptions it may very well have been the masterpiece of its genre. It was probably more warmly received than his shorter poems because of its representation of classical myths. Unlike most of his poetry, it is not as readily accessible to a modern audience.

Catullus presented his ancient audience with poetry that ignored popular expectations in subject matter and style. He stripped away what was not essential or had lost its vibrancy. Catullus' ancient audience would naturally have been threatened by this change. We too would be threatened by real change in contemporary writing, if we were not living in what Frye has called the 'chaotic age' in literature. We have been treated to so much shock art from one-letter-per-page literature to meat dresses, that the attempt to shock is cliché. The modernists, Eliot, Pound, and Williams, following Victorian and Edwardian poetry so closely, provide a loose comparison to Catullus' circle and the considerable change they proposed from their Roman predecessors.

Translators always lose something of the original. As Robert Frost said, 'poetry is what is lost in translation.' In response to that dictum, Borges claimed in his lecture on verse translation, that Steffan George's German translations of Baudelaire are more skillful than Baudelaire's original poems in French. That does not make George a better poet. It is Baudelaire we feel we are reading in German, not George. It is also clear that George is less interesting than the poets he translated.

I think of a translation as a possible reading of an original work translator has chosen the angle of our line of sight. With luck and alchemy they choose well, although something will always be missing.

In this volume, I have tried to remain as close as possible to the spirit of Catullus. Some previous translations are very good but they cannot escape the time in which they were written. Some are very accurate but not poetic. Some stray far from the original. Others are rhymed and are not poetic when read aloud in English, almost all soften the humour of the original. These are the particular and inevitable vices of translators and their time. No doubt translators will point out my deficiencies, but I hope it will be done in the spirit of Catullus.

Ewan Whyte,
Toronto, 2004

POEMS

I.

CVI dono lepidum nouum libellum
arida modo pumice expolitum?
Corneli, tibi: namque tu solebas
meas esse aliquid putare nugas
iam tum, cum ausus es unus Italorum
omne aeuum tribus explicare cartis
doctis, Iuppiter, et laboriosis.
quare habe tibi quidquid hoc libelli
qualecumque; quod, patrona virgo
plus uno maneat perenne saeclo.

1.

Who shall I give my new little
book just polished clean and pretty
with pumice? To Corneilius,
you who said my scrawls were worth
a second look, back when you alone
of the Romans were bold enough
to write a history of the
world in one very large book,
a remarkable labour. I give it
to you to keep as your own.
O Muse! by your gifts may it be
good enough to last a hundred years.

II.

PASSER, deliciae meae puellae,
quicum ludere, quem in sinu tenere,
cui primum digitum dare appetenti
et acris solet incitare morsus,
cum desiderio meo nitenti
carum nescio quid lubet iocari
et solaciolum sui doloris,
credo ut tum grauis acquiescat ardor:
tecum ludere sicut ipsa possem
et tristis animi leuare curas!

2.

Sparrow, my Lesbia's pet that she holds
between her breasts and lets flutter
in her hands and on her head, laughing
as he chirps coming to her again
and again. She teases him with her
fingertips, earning stinging pecks to
her delight. I wish I could dampen my
desire for her by playing with you, little
sparrow. I would dream of her naked smell
through your pecks to quench my miseries.

III.

LVGETE, o Veneres Cupidinesque,
et quantum est hominum uenustiorum:
passer mortuus est meae puellae,
passer, deliciae meae puellae,
quem plus illa oculis suis amabat.
nam mellitus erat suamque norat
ipsam tam bene quam puella matrem,
nec sese a gremio illius mouebat,
sed circumsiliens modo huc modo illuc
ad solam dominam usque pipiabat.
qui nunc it per iter tenebricosum
illuc, unde negant redire quemquam.
at uobis male sit, malae tenebrae
Orci, quae omnia bella deuoratis:
tam bellum mihi passerem abstulistis
o factum male! o miselle passer!
tua nunc opera meae puellae
flendo turgiduli rubent ocelli.

3.

O Venus and longing Sorrow,
my Lesbia's sparrow is dead!
He was her delight. Tears
are wetting her cheeks
for she loved him more than
her eyes. For her, he was
sweeter than honey. He
thought she was his mother,
hopping on her head,
playing with her hair;
now he has passed to
the dark shadows from where
there is no return. Orcus,
destroyer of all beauty,
has stolen from me my beautiful
sparrow and now my Lesbia's eyes
are swollen red with tears.

IV.

PHASELVS ille, quem uidetis, hospites,
ait fuisse nauium celerrimus,
neque ullius natantis impetum trabis
nequisse praeterire, siue palmulis
opus foret uolare siue linteo.
et hoc negat minacis Hadriatici
negare litus insulasue Cycladas
Rhodumque nobilem horridamque Thraciam
Propontida trucemue Ponticum sinum,
ubi iste post phaselus antea fuit
comata silua; nam Cytorio in iugo
loquente saepe sibilum edidit coma.
Amastri Pontica et Cytore buxifer,
tibi haec fuisse et esse cognitissima
ait phaselus: ultima ex origine
tuo stetisse dicit in cacumine,
tuo imbuisse palmulas in aequore,
et inde tot per impotentia freta
erum tulisse, laeua siue dextera
uocaret aura, siue utrumque Iuppiter
simul secundus incidisset in pedem;
neque ulla uota litoralibus deis
sibi esse facta, cum ueniret a mari
nouissimo hunc ad usque limpidum lacum.
sed haec prius fuere: nunc recondita
senet quiete seque dedicat tibi,
gemelle Castor et gemelle Castoris.

4.

My friends, the vessel you see
before you was once faster than
anything on the surface of the
water with oar or sail. She claims
the shores of the hostile Adriatic
and the rough Cyclades will concede
this. She knew the waters off noble
Rhodes, the Propontos, and the Pontic
Gulf where she was once a great tree
high on mount Cytorus. There she gave
voice through her leaves. She still
remembers her oars when they first
wetted the sea. She carried her master
safely across great distances
at his control, whether the wind fell
against her or, by Jupiter's favour,
directly behind. Never were there
prayers to the gods for shore when
storms overtook her. Now she
rests on these shallow waters.
In her great age she devotes
herself to the twin gods, patrons
of vessels, and remembers.

V.

VIVAMUS mea Lesbia, atque amemus,
rumoresque senum seueriorum
omnes unius aestimemus assis!
soles occidere et redire possunt:
nobis cum semel occidit breuis lux,
nox est perpetua una dormienda.
da mi basia mille, deinde centum,
dein mille altera, dein secunda centum,
deinde usque altera mille, deinde centum.
dein, cum milia multa fecerimus,
conturbabimus illa, ne sciamus,
aut ne quis malus inuidere possit,
cum tantum sciat esse basiorum.

5.

Let us live and love,
not listening to old men's talk.
Suns will rise and set
long after our little light
has gone away to darkness.
Kiss me again and again.
Let me kiss you a hundred times,
a thousand more, again a thousand
without rest, losing count, so no
one can speak of us and say
they know the number of our kisses.

VI.

FLAVI, delicias tuas Catullo,
ni sint illepidae atque inelegantes,
uelles dicere nec tacere posses.
uerum nescio quid febriculosi
scorti diligis: hoc pudet fateri.
nam te non uiduas iacere noctes
nequiquam tacitum cubile clamat
sertis ac Syrio fragrans oliuo,
puluinusque peraeque et hic et ille
attritus, tremulique quassa lecti
argutatio inambulatioque.
nam inista preualet nihil tacere.
cur? non tam latera ecfututa pandas,
ni tu quid facias ineptiarum.
quare, quidquid habes boni malique,
dic nobis. uolo te ac tuos amores
ad caelum lepido uocare uersu.

6.

Flavius, you're not telling
your Catullus of your love.
You think I don't know she's
a cheap whore. You are
embarrassed! Your bed with
its Syrian oils and leaves
does not speak of you lying
alone at night. You cannot
silence the creaks and jostlings
of your bed. Your indented
pillows prove you are up to
something. Why do you hide your
actions? Tell me everything!
I want to describe your deeds
joyfully to the Heavens in verse!

VII.

QVAERIS, quot mihi basiationes
tuae, Lesbia, sint satis superque.
quam magnus numerus Libyssae harenae
lasarpiciferis iacet Cyrenis
oraclum Iouis inter aestuosi
et Batti ueteris sacrum sepulcrum;
aut quam sidera multa, cum tacet nox,
furtiuos hominum uident amores:
tam te basia multa basiare
uesano satis et super Catullo est,
quae nec pernumerare curiosi
possint nec mala fascinare lingua.

7.

Lesbia, you ask me how many
of your kisses are enough
for you to save for me?
As many as there are grains of sand
in the African desert!
As many as the winds that
blow on the shores of Cyrene
where Silphium grows between
King Battus' sacred tomb
and Jupiter Amons Oracle.
As many kisses as there
are stars in the night
that shine on all men's
secrets. After all of these
your Catullus will have
enough kisses for a while,
enough that clever eyes
can not tell the number
and slanderous tongues are
counting so they are mute.

VIII.

MISER Catulle, desinas ineptire,
et quod uides perisse perditum ducas.
fulsere quondam candidi tibi soles,
cum uentitabas quo puella ducebat
amata nobis quantum amabitur nulla.
ibi illa multa cum iocosa fiebant,
quae tu uolebas nec puella nolebat,
fulsere uere candidi tibi soles.
nunc iam illa non uult: tu quoque impotens noli,
nec quae fugit sectare, nec miser uiue,
sed obstinata mente perfer, obdura.
uale puella, iam Catullus obdurat,
nec te requiret nec rogabit inuitam.
at tu dolebis, cum rogaberis nulla.
scelesta, uae te, quae tibi manet uita?
quis nunc te adibit? cui uideberis bella?
quem nunc amabis? cuius esse diceris?
quem basiabis? cui labella mordebis?
at tu, Catulle, destinatus obdura.

8.

Unfortunate Catullus
cease your foolishness.
Accept your loss.
The bright lights of
happiness used to shine
on you when you loved
your Lesbia as no woman
ever was loved. She would
lead you by the hand
and you followed wherever
she wanted to take you.
Her laughter is all gone
she no longer wants you.
You are powerless to change
this. You must not want her.
Don't chase her. Try to be
happy. Be cold to her in
return. Catullus will be
strong since she no longer
wants him. I hope it will
hurt you when you see
you are not pursued
"Tart! Off with you!"
What will you do with
yourself? Who will visit
you? Who will still want
your beauty when they
know your tricks? Who do
you kiss now? Who bites
your lips? Who do you love?
Foolish Catullus, you
must be strong for once.

IX.

VERANI, omnibus e meis amicis
antistans mihi milibus trecentis,
uenistine domum ad tuos penates
fratresque unanimos anumque matrem?
uenisti. o mihi nuntii beati!
uisam te incolumem audiamque Hiberum
narrantem loca, facta nationes,
ut mos est tuus, applicansque collum
iucundum os oculosque suauiabor.
o quantum est hominum beatiorum,
quid me laetius est beatiusue?

9.

Veranius, more dear to me than all my friends,
even if I had three hundred thousand.
By the guardian Gods have you truly come back
home to see your frail mother and loving brothers?
You have come back! Great news for me!
I will see you alive and well and hear your talk
of far off lands, the sights of Iberia and strange
tribes. I shall kiss your eyelids, before hearing
your wonderful stories long into the night.

X.

VARVS me meus ad suos amores
uisum duxerat e foro otiosum,
scortillum, ut mihi tum repente uisum est,
non sane illepidum neque inuenustum,
huc ut uenimus, incidere nobis
sermones uarii, in quibus, quid esset
iam Bithynia, quo modo se haberet,
et quonam mihi profuisset aere.
respondi id quod erat, nihil neque ipsis
nec praetoribus esse nec cohorti,
cur quisquam caput unctius referret,
praesertim quibus esset irrumator
praetor, nec faceret pili cohortem.
'at certe tamen,' inquiunt 'quod illic
natum dicitur esse, comparasti
ad lecticam homines.' ego, ut puellae
unum me facerem beatiorem,
'non' inquam 'mihi tam fuit maligne
ut, prouincia quod mala incidisset,
non possem octo homines parare rectos.'
at mi nullus erat nec hic neque illic
fractum qui ueteris pedem grabati
in collo sibi collocare posset.
hic illa, ut decuit cinaediorem,
'quaeso' inquit 'mihi, mi Catulle, paulum
istos commoda: nam uolo ad Serapim
deferri.' 'mane' inquii puellae,
'istud quod modo dixeram me habere,
fugit me ratio: meus sodalis—
Cinna est Gaius— is sibi parauit.
uerum, utrum illius an mei, quid ad me?
utor tam bene quam mihi pararim.
sed tu insulsa male et molesta uiuis,
per quam non licet esse neglegentem.'

10.

Verus pulled me aside dragging me away
from the Forum to see his lover, a cute
prostitute, not lacking in grace.
We started talking about various things
before she asked how things were in Bithynia,
"Did you come back with any money from your
visit?" I told her the truth: "None of us,
not even the Praeters, who screwed us all,
came back with a fancy hair-do.
If they did not get rich, you can be
sure no employees did." She said, "But you
must have been carried around in a litter –
it's natural there." I said, wanting to feel
important, "Oh that, as bad as the province
was, it's not hard to find eight healthy men to cart you
around in a litter. I even brought them back."
She then, like the cheap tart she was,
said, "Please, Catullus, lend me those men
and that litter so I can ride to the temple
of Serapis." I told her I borrowed them.
'They are Gaius Cinnas's. He said to use them
as though they are my own. I won't take the
trouble of believing him. Besides, if I lent
them to you, you might run someone over!"

XI.

FVRI et Aureli comites Catulli,
siue in extremos penetrabit Indos,
litus ut longe resonante Eoa
tunditur unda,

siue in Hyrcanos Arabesue molles,
seu Sagas sagittiferosue Parthos,
siue quae septemgeminus colorat
aequora Nilus,

siue trans altas gradietur Alpes,
Caesaris uisens monimenta magni,
Gallicum Rhenum horribile aequor ulti
mosque Britannos,

omnia haec, quaecumque feret uoluntas
caelitum, temptare simul parati,
pauca nuntiate meae puellae
non bona dicta.

cum suis uiuat ualeatque moechis,
quos simul complexa tenet trecentos,
nullum amans uere, sed identidem omnium
ilia rumpens;

nec meum respectet, ut ante, amorem,
qui illius culpa cecidit uelut prati
ultimi flos, praetereunte postquam
tactus aratro est.

11.

Fureus and Aurelius, loyal
friends, they would accompany
me to the outermost reaches of
India where the shore clashes with
the resounding waves of the dawn

or to the land of Hyrcania, or
Arabia, or even to Sacia, or among
the archer Parthians, or to where the
seven-mouthed Nile colours the sea.

They would even cross the high Alps
to gaze upon the deeds of Caesar,
the cold Gallic Rhine or remote
Britain. They are resolved to
try all this at once or whatever
else the gods might will.

I asked them to tell my Lesbia a few
parting words, though they are not
very good. May she live very well
with her new batch of lovers, however
many hundred they may be. May she
embrace three hundred at once.

May none of them truly love her, may she
rupture them from repetition. May she
never be able to look back on my love,
which she has killed by her carelessness
as a wild flower growing on a field's
edge is grazed by a passing plow.

XIII.

CENABIS bene, mi Fabulle, apud me
paucis, si tibi di fauent, diebus,
si tecum attuleris bonam atque magnam
cenam, non sine candida puella
et uino et sale et omnibus cachinnis.
haec si, inquam, attuleris, uenuste noster,
cenabis bene; nam tui Catulli
plenus sacculus est aranearum.
sed contra accipies meros amores
seu quid suauius elegantiusue est:
nam unguentum dabo, quod meae puellae
donarunt Veneres Cupidinesque,
quod tu cum olfacies, deos rogabis,
totum ut te faciant, Fabulle, nasum.

13.

Fabullius, my dear friend, in a short time
you will feast with me in my own house—
if the gods will allow it. But you will
have to supply the feast, the wine,
the beautiful girls, the laughter
and the wit brought by their presence.
My feast depends on this since the purse
where I used to keep my coins is now
the home of a spider, but at your feast
I will present you with a lotion
from my Lesbia given to her by
a priestess of Venus. When you
smell it, Fabullius, you will wish
to the gods you were a giant nose.

XVII.

O Colonia, quae cupis ponte ludere longo,
et salire paratum habes, sed uereris inepta
crura ponticuli axulis stantis in rediuiuis,
ne supinus eat cauaque in palude recumbat:
sic tibi bonus ex tua pons libidine fiat,
in quo uel Salisubsali sacra suscipiantur,
munus hoc mihi maximi da, Colonia, risus.
quendam municipem meum de tuo uolo ponte
ire praecipitem in lutum per caputque pedesque,
uerum totius ut lacus putidaeque paludis
liuidissima maximeque est profunda uorago.
insulsissimus est homo, nec sapit pueri instar
bimuli tremula patris dormientis in ulna.
cui cum sit uiridissimo nupta flore puella
et puella tenellulo delicatior haedo,
adseruanda nigerrimis diligentius uuis,
ludere hanc sinit ut lubet, nec pili facit uni,
nec se subleuat ex sua parte, sed uelut alnus
in fossa Liguri iacet suppernata securi, •
tantundem omnia sentiens quam si nulla sit usquam;
talis iste meus stupor nil uidet, nihil audit,
ipse qui sit, utrum sit an non sit, id quoque nescit.
nunc eum uolo de tuo ponte mittere pronum,
si pote stolidum repente excitare ueternum,
et supinum animum in graui derelinquere caeno,
ferream ut soleam tenaci in uoragine mula.

17.

O Verona, my city, you
wish to dance and play
on a new stone bridge.
One that is fit for public
festivals, rather than your
rickety wooden bridge that
leans toward the slime below.
May you have a new bridge
and may it be strong enough
for the festival of the Salii
whose thunder is fierce
dancing feet in the night.
O Verona, if you could
help me with one thing,
it would make everyone laugh.
There is a man of this town
that I would watch with joy
if he went somersaulting
from your new bridge
into the thickest part of
the slime. He is a remarkable
ass who has less sense
than a two-year old sleeping
in his father's arms.
He is married to a girl
who is like the first leaves
of spring, she needs to be
guarded as though she were a
baby goat poking its nose into
everything and running wildly,
or ripe grapes the day before
the harvest. He can't be bothered
to watch her. He believes everything
she tells him. The dense cuckold
is like an alder bush hacked down
and tossed in a ditch. He is the one
I want thrown off your new bridge.
The vigorous experience might wake
him out of his living sleep, as
a mule climbs from the thick
mud leaving his iron shoes behind.

Catullus

XXV.

CINAEDE Thalle, mollior cuniculi capillo
uel anseris medullula uel imula oricilla
uel pene languido senis situque araneoso,
idemque, Thalle, turbida rapacior procella,
cum diua mulier aries ostendit oscitantes,
remitte pallium mihi meum, quod inuolasti,
sudariumque Saetabum catagraphosque Thynos,
inepte, quae palam soles habere tamquam auita.
quae nunc tuis ab unguibus reglutina et remitte,
ne laneum latusculum manusque mollicellas
inusta turpiter tibi flagella conscribillent,
et insolenter aestues, uelut minuta magno
deprensa nauis in mari, uesaniente uento.

25.

Thallus, you nasty little sodomite,
you're softer than rabbits' fur, softer
than goose marrow or the gentle flesh of
earlobes, you're softer than an old
man's flopping penis and the spider
webs growing there. Thallus, you're
greedier than the wind in a fierce storm
making off with whatever's not nailed down.
Give me back my coat, my Saetaban napkin,
and my Thynian tablets you cart
around saying they are your family heirlooms,
or else I will thrash your grasping hands
and your fat little ass 'til you twist
and turn like a small boat caught in
my great storm on the open sea.

XXVI.

FVRI, uillula vestra non ad Austri
flatus opposita est neque ad Fauoni
nec saeui Boreae aut Apheliotae,
uerum ad milia quindecim et ducentos.
o uentum horribilem atque pestilentem!

26.

Furius, your little villa trembles,
but not from the cold north wind
or the east wind that tears ships
apart on the open sea or terrible
storms from thunder-hurling Jupiter,
but from a chilling fifteen
thousand Sesterces debt which rains
pestilence on your imagination.

XXVII.

MINISTER uetuli puer Falerni
inger mi calices amariores,
ut lex Postumiae iubet magistrae
ebriosa acina ebriosioris.
at uos quo lubet hinc abite, lymphae
uini pernicies, et ad seueros
migrate. hic merus est Thyonianus.

27.

Come waiter, give me the best falernian
wine! Tonight our host Postumia is
drunker than the vine that grew the
grape. I know she wants you to give
us water now, but give me the real
thing. Don't throw water on the fire
which Bacchus gives for our delight.

XXXI.

PAENE insularum, Sirmio, insularumque
ocelle, quascumque in liquentibus stagnis
marique uasto fert uterque Neptunus,
quam te libenter quamque laetus inuiso,
uix mi ipse credens Thuniam atque Bithunos
liquisse campos et uidere te in tuto.
o quid solutis est beatius curis,
cum mens onus reponit, ac peregrino
labore fessi uenimus larem ad nostrum,
desideratoque acquiescimus lecto?
hoc est quod unum est pro laboribus tantis.
salue, o uenusta Sirmio, atque ero gaude
gaudente, uosque, o Lydiae lacus undae,
ridete quidquid est domi cachinnorum.

31.

Little Sirmio, of all islands
and islets, you are my jewel,
graceful, beside Neptune's
clear waters. With what joy
I come to see you. Rough
Thrace and the flat plains
of Bithynia are only a memory
left far behind. Now I see you
once again, quiet and safe.
Exile and travel have given
me a desire for your beauty.
O Sirmio, rejoice at your master's
return and let the laughter of
my home echo to distant Lydia.

XXXII.

AMABO, mea dulcis Ipsitilla,
meae deliciae, mei lepores,
iube ad te ueniam meridiatum.
et si iusseris, illud adiuuato,
ne quis liminis obseret tabellam,
neu tibi lubeat foras abire,
sed domi maneas paresque nobis
nouem continuas fututiones.
uerum si quid ages, statim iubeto:
nam pransus iaceo et satur supinus
pertundo tunicamque palliumque.

32.

Ipsitilla my sweet
and luscious tart,
ask me to come by at noon.
If you grant me this,
grant me one thing more.
Leave your door unlocked.
Please don't step out,
but prepare for us
a nine course feast of love.
Please send me news at once
for now I lie on my back
and my desire is poking
through the covers bumping
into my breakfast plate.

XXXIII.

O FVRVM optime balneariorum
Vibenni pater et cinaede fili
(nam dextra pater inquinatiore,
culo filius est uoraciore),
cur non exilium malasque in oras
itis? quandoquidem patris rapinae
notae sunt populo, et natis pilosas,
fili, non potes asse uenditare.

33.

Vibennius, most grasping of bath house
thieves, stealing even the clothes of
the unfortunate. Even your son has
inherited your grasping instinct, but
he clutches only with his buttocks.
Both of you ought to go to hell
or at least into exile; for the
people now know what you are up to
and your son is so ugly he can't
even sell his hairy ass for a meal.

XXXIV.

DIANAE sumus in fide
puellae et pueri integri:
Dianam pueri integri
puellaeque canamus.
o Latonia, maximi
magna progenies Iouis,
quam mater prope Deliam
deposiuit oliuam,
montium domina ut fores
siluarumque uirentium
saltuumque reconditorum
amniumque sonantum:
tu Lucina dolentibus
Iuno dicta puerperis,
tu potens Triuia et notho es
dicta lumine Luna.
tu cursu, dea, menstruo
metiens iter annuum,
rustica agricolae bonis
tecta frugibus exples.
sis quocumque tibi placet
sancta nomine, Romulique,
antique ut solita es, bona
sospites ope gentem.

34.

Diana, we girls and boys
offer our praises to you,
honouring you with hymns
of sweetest song. O Latona's
great child, daughter of
greatest Jove, she gave
birth to you in Delius's
sacred grove, declaring your
rule of mountains and
sequestered woods, patron
of hills and streams. Lucina,
bringer of light and childbirth,
borrower of the rays of the
moon, women call to you in
their birth pains for salve.
Swift goddess, you who measure
the months of the year, and
give the farmer the rich
fruits of the harvest, we
invoke you and your protection
through one of your many names.
Help us now as you have always
loved the sons of Romulus.

XXXIX.

EGNATIVS, quod candidos habet dentes,
renidet usque quaque. si ad rei uentum est
subsellium, cum orator excitat fletum,
renidet ille; si ad pii rogum fili
lugetur, orba cum flet unicum mater,
renidet ille. quidquid est, ubicumque est,
quodcumque agit, renidet: hunc habet morbum,
neque elegantem, ut arbitror, neque urbanum.
quare monendum est te mihi, bone Egnati.
si urbanus esses aut Sabinus aut Tiburs
aut pinguis Vmber aut obesus Etruscus
aut Lanuuinus ater atque dentatus
aut Transpadanus, ut meos quoque attingam,
aut quilubet, qui puriter lauit dentes,
tamen renidere usque quaque te nollem:
nam risu inepto res ineptior nulla est.
nunc Celtiber es: Celtiberia in terra,
quod quisque minxit, hoc sibi solet mane
dentem atque russam defricare gingiuam,
ut quo iste uester expolitior dens est,
hoc te amplius bibisse praedicet loti.

39.

Egnatius, you are proud of your shiny white
teeth. You are always smiling whether it is
appropriate or not. In court, when devastating
evidence is given, you smile. At a funeral pyre,
where a mother weeps for her only son, you smile.
Wherever you are or whomever you are with, you
never hesitate to show your shiny teeth. This
inveterate habit shows you have no class.
You should know one thing, Egnatius. Wherever
you are from, if from a city or the Sabine,
or the banks of the Tiber, or even if you were
an Umbrian pig or round Etruscan or dark Lanuvian,
or a Transpadine like myself, you think men will
think of you as a man who is clean and washes
his teeth with fresh water in the morning.
But to tell you the truth, and to wipe your
incessant smile from your face: in Rome it
is well known, that Celt-Iberians, of which they
say you are one, keep their teeth white by washing
them every morning with their own piss. And your
own grin proclaims what you have been drinking.

XLI.

AMEANA puella defututa
tota milia me decem poposcit,
ista turpiculo puella naso,
decoctoris amica Formiani.
propinqui, quibus est puella curae,
amicos medicosque conuocate:
non est sana puella, nec rogare
qualis sit solet aes imaginosum.

41.

Ameana, exhausted tart with an awful
nose, I can't believe you just begged
me for ten thousand. Will you give me
the lay of a lifetime for it? You are
mad. Call your friends over, your
wretched boyfriend and a good doctor.
Your wretched face would scare a
mirror if ever you cared to look at one.

XLVI.

IAM uer egelidos refert tepores,
iam caeli furor aequinoctialis
iucundis Zephyri silescit aureis.
linquantur Phrygii, Catulle, campi
Nicaeaeque ager uber aestuosae:
ad claras Asiae uolemus urbes.
iam mens praetrepidans auet uagari,
iam laeti studio pedes uigescunt.
o dulces comitum ualete coetus,
longe quos simul a domo profectos
diuersae uarie uiae reportant.

46.

Now the spring warms the sleepy earth
and the skies are calmed by the west
wind. It is time to leave Phrygia, Catullus,
and the rich plains of Nicaea and its
fierce heat. Go to the famous cities of
Asia. My mind is eager and my feet dance
at the thought of travel. My friends, with
sadness I say goodbye, far from Rome — where
on different paths, we all seek to return.

XLVII.

PORCI et Socration, duae sinistrae
Pisonis, scabies famesque mundi,
uos Veraniolo meo et Fabullo
uerpus praeposuit Priapus ille?
uos conuiuia lauta sumptuose
de die facitis, mei sodales
quaerunt in triuio uocationes?

47.

Porcius and Socraton,
the twin left hands,
greed and corruption,
feast at the side
of Piso the Consul.
While my dear friends
Fabulus and Veranius
are kept away.
Luscious feasts and
gardens are no longer
open to you. Beautiful guests
ignore you. Now
you have to linger
around cross-roads
looking for a meal.

IL.

DISERTISSIME Romuli nepotum,
quot sunt quotque fuere, Marce Tulli,
quotque post aliis erunt in annis,
gratias tibi maximas Catullus
agit pessimus omnium poeta,
tanto pessimus omnium poeta,
quanto tu optimus omnium patronus.

49.

The highest praise of the sons
of Romulus who have come before,
and those yet to come, is yours for
eloquence Marcus Tullius. Catullus,
worst of poets, offers you his
gratitude. The worst of poets as
you are the greatest of Orators.

L.

HESTERNO, Licini, die otiosi
multum lusimus in meis tabellis,
ut conuenerat esse delicatos:
scribens uersiculos uterque nostrum
ludebat numero modo hoc modo illoc,
reddens mutua per iocum atque uinum.
atque illinc abii tuo lepore
incensus, Licini, facetiisque,
ut nec me miserum cibus iuuaret
nec somnus tegeret quiete ocellos,
sed toto indomitus furore lecto
uersarer, cupiens uidere lucem,
ut tecum loquerer, simulque ut essem.
at defessa labore membra postquam
semimortua lectulo iacebant,
hoc, iucunde, tibi poema feci,
ex quo perspiceres meum dolorem.
nunc audax caue sis, precesque nostras,
oramus, caue despuas, ocelle,
ne poenas Nemesis reposcat a te.
est uehemens dea: laedere hanc caueto.

50.

Yesterday, Licinius, to pass some
time, we took my tablets and played
a game of rude Epigrams, taking
turns writing line after line,
playing with rhythm and metre,
drinking wine and laughing.
When I left you, your wit stayed
with me and I could not sleep or
eat, tossing in my bed, waiting for
the day so I could try to see you
again. Finally, at dawn when I
was half-dead with exhaustion,
I wrote this poem for you.
Please come and talk to me,
you can see my pain and that
poetry is a nourishment to
me. Don't be too proud, for
Nemesis, goddess of revenge,
may gently haunt you for it,
and you cannot hide from her wit.

LII.

QVID est, Catulle? quid moraris emori?
sella in curuli struma Nonius sedet,
per consulatum peierat Vatinius:
quid est, Catulle? quid moraris emori?

52.

Why, Catullus, do you not consider
your own funeral? Put an end to it
all. Nonius, the parasite, now holds
high office and will sell Vatinius
the consulship. Don't wait to be
fed to the lions, end it all now.

LIII.

RISI nescio quem modo e corona,
qui, cum mirifice Vatiniana
meus crimina Caluos explicasset
admirans ait haec manusque tollens,
'di magni, salaputium disertum!'

53.

My dear Calvus, when you were in the open forum
listing off the crimes of Vatinius to the crowd,
your eloquence rose to magnificent style.
I was crippled with laughter when a man yelled,
"The gods have a thunder-tongued midget!"

LIV.

OTHONIS caput oppido est pusillum,
et eri rustice semilauta crura,
subtile et leue peditum Libonis,
si non omnia, displicere uellem
tibi et Sufficio seni recocto...
irascere iterum meis iambis
inmerentibus, unice imperator.

54.

Otho, you have a very small head and your
brain, no doubt, wanders in that tiny space.
Erius, your delicate, unwashed legs attract
dogs eager to relieve themselves. Libo,
the rotting smell of your wet farts
clears the crowd as though you were a
passing god. Fulficus, you senile goat,
marshal of fools, these things don't offend
you; so why are you offended by my verse?

LVI.

O REM ridiculam, Cato, et iocosam,
dignamque auribus et tuo cachinno!
ride quidquid amas, Cato, Catullum:
res est ridicula et nimis iocosa.
deprendi modo pupulum puellae
trusantem; hunc ego, si placet Dionae,
protelo rigida mea cecidi.

56.

Cato, a thing of outrageous humour just
occurred, it is extremely funny. As you
love your Catullus, you will laugh.
Half hidden, I came upon a young man,
servicing his girlfriend. I noticed my
own erection and baring all, I leapt on
them, while pleading the forgiveness of Venus!

LVII.

PVLCRE conuenit improbis cinaedis,
Mamurrae pathicoque Caesarique.
nec mirum: maculae pares utrisque,
urbana altera et illa Formiana,
impressae resident nec eluentur:
morbosi pariter, gemelli utrique,
uno in lecticulo erudituli ambo,
non hic quam ille magis uorax adulter,
riuales socii puellularum.
pulcre conuenit improbis cinaedis.

57.

They are a beautiful pair, Mamura and
Caesar, sleeping with everyone in sight.
And when no one else is willing, with each
other. Is it any surprise, they caught
the same disease? One caught it in the city,
the other in the country. Whatever the case,
there is no cure for them. Rivals in the
quantities of other men's wives, the
literary pair are screwing almost without
cease. A beautiful pair, Mamura and Caesar.

LVIII.

CAELI, Lesbia nostra, Lesbia illa.
illa Lesbia, quam Catullus unam
plus quam se atque suos amauit omnes,
nunc in quadriuiis et angiportis
glubit magnanimi Remi nepotes.

58.

Lesbia, whom I loved more
than myself and more than
any of my dearest; my Lesbia,
whom I held more precious
than life, now lingers around
cross-roads and alleyways
tugging on the cocks
of Rome's mighty sons.

LVIIIb.

NON custos si fingar ille Cretum,
non Ladas ego pinnipesue Perseus,
non si Pegaseo ferar uolatu,
non Rhesi niueae citaeque bigae;
adde huc plumipedas uolatilesque,
uentorumque simul require cursum,
quos iunctos, Cameri, mihi dicares:
defessus tamen omnibus medullis
et multis languoribus peresus
essem te mihi, amice, quaeritando.

58B.

Not if I were Talus, the man of
bronze whose giant height could
see over all Crete, not if
I were Ladas, swift-footed
messenger of Alexander, or the
wing-footed hero Perseus. Not
if I were given the flight
of Pegasus or the twin
horses of Rhesus, the winds,
and all manner of flight.
I would still be exhausted
in my search for you Camerius.

LIX.

BONONIENSIS Rufa Rufulum fellat,
uxor Meneni, saepe quam in sepulcretis
uidistis ipso rapere de rogo cenam,
cum deuolutum ex igne prosequens panem
ab semiraso tunderetur ustore.

59.

Rufia, the wife of Menenius,
is blowing Rufulus. She is quite
a prize. You can see her in cemeteries
looking like a mourner, stealing the
sacred food placed for the dead
or chasing a loaf of bread as it
rolls off the funeral pyre, before
being beaten away by a half-shaved
corpse-burner who knows her by name.

LX.

NVM te leaena montibus Libystinis
aut Scylla latrans infima inguinum parte
tam mente dura procreauit ac taetra,
ut supplicis uocem in nouissimo casu
contemptam haberes, a nimis fero corde?

60.

A lioness from the mountains of Libya
must have given birth to you, or the great
monster Scylla whose voice is the howling
of dogs; for how else can your cruelty be
accounted for? I am dying. Your contempt
knows no bounds. Your heart is turned
away and you have no ear for my words.

LXI.

COLLIS o Heliconii
cultor, Vraniae genus,
qui rapis teneram ad uirum
uirginem, o Hymenaee Hymen,
ó Hymen Hymenaee;
cinge tempora floribus
suaue olentis amaraci,
flammeum cape laetus, huc
huc ueni, niueo gerens
luteum pede soccum;
excitusque hilari die,
nuptialia concinens
uoce carmina tinnula,
pelle humum pedibus, manu
pineam quate taedam.
namque Iunia Manlio,
qualis Idalium colens
uenit ad Phrygium Venus
iudicem, bona cum bona
nubet alite uirgo,
floridis uelut enitens
myrtus Asia ramulis
quos Hamadryades deae
ludicrum sibi roscido
nutriunt umore.
quare age, huc aditum ferens,
perge linquere Thespiae
rupis Aonios specus,
nympha quos super irrigat
frigerans Aganippe.
ac domum dominam uoca
coniugis cupidam noui,
mentem amore reuinciens,
ut tenax hedera huc et huc
arborem implicat errans.
uosque item simul, integrae
uirgines, quibus aduenit
par dies, agite in modum

61.

Keeper of Helicon's hill
son of the planetary wonders.
You carry the young
bride to the bridegroom.
O Hymen, Hymenae,
O Hymen, Hymenae!
Tie amaricus flowers
around your head.
Wrap your body with your
ritual robe,
before you come here
on golden winged sandals.
Light the joyful fires
singing wedding hymns
with your powerful voice.
Pound the earth with your feet
swinging your torch in the air.
Idalian Venus, as beautiful as
you were when you persuaded
the Trojan to choose your gift
unknowingly creating war,
so is Arunculeias' radiance
as she comes to marry her
Manlius. The gift of the augers
tell us of your goodness
and the flights of the birds
prove it, as Asian myrtle in
the bright sun tended by
wood nymphs with nightly
dew brings joy to all.
Come quickly. Leave
your Aonian cave
and thespian cliffs
where Aganapies stream
pours herself over the
cold hills and rocks.

dicite, o Hymenaee Hymen,
o Hymen Hymenaee.
ut libentius, audiens
se citarier ad suum
munus, huc aditum ferat
. dux bonae Veneris, boni
coniugator amoris.
quis deus magis est amatis
petendus amantibus?
quem colent homines magis
caelitum, o Hymenaee Hymen,
o Hymen Hymenaee?
te suis tremulus parens
inuocat, tibi uirgines
zonula soluunt sinus,
te timens cupida nouos
captat aure maritus.
tu fero iuueni in manus
floridam ipse puellulam
dedis a gremio suae
matris, o Hymenaee Hymen,
o Hymen Hymenaee.
nil potest sine te Venus,
fama quod bona comprobet,
commodi capere, at potest
te uolente. quis huic deo
compararier ausit?
nulla quit sine te domus
liberos dare, nec parens
stirpe nitier; ac potest
te uolente. quis huic deo
compararier ausit?
quae tuis careat sacris,
non queat dare praesides
terra finibus: at queat
te uolente. quis huic deo
compararier ausit?
claustra pandite ianuae.
uirgo adest. uiden ut faces
splendidas quatiunt comas?

Arunculeia desires for her
future husband and a home.
Wrap ivy leaves around her
and her Manlius making them
a single tree. Give voice
together women and girls
still unwed, for you know
a day like this awaits you.
O Hymen, Hymenae,
O Hymen, Hymenae!
True to his duties he will
come when he is called.
An honourable god of love
to unite true lovers. What
god is better for earnest
lovers to seek? Of all the gods,
who receives the most prayers?
O Hymenae, Hymen,
O Hymen, Hymenae!
All fathers invoke you for
their children. For you,
virgins open themselves,
though the bridegroom
listens in fear. You give
the bride from her mother's
arms her flowering beauty taken
by the rough-handed bridegroom
O Hymenae, Hymen,
O Hymen, Hymenae!
Venus can do nothing
honourable without you
only with you has she her
full powers. What god is
comparable to you? Hold
open the gates, she is here.
The torches shake their
bright locks of fire.

* * * * * * *
* * * * * * *
* * * * * * *
* * * * * * *

tardet ingenuus pudor.
quem tamen magis audiens,
flet quod ire necesse est.
flere desine. non tibi Aurunculeia
periculum est,
ne qua femina pulcrior
clarum ab Oceano diem
uiderit uenientem.
talis in uario solet
diuitis domini hortulo
stare flos hyacinthinus.
sed moraris, abit dies.
prodeas noua nupta.
prodeas noua nupta, si
iam uidetur, et audias
nostra uerba. uiden? faces
aureas quatiunt comas:
prodeas noua nupta.
non tuus leuis in mala
deditus uir adultera,
probra turpia persequens,
a tuis teneris uolet
secubare papillis,
lenta sed uelut adsitas
uitis implicat arbores,
implicabitur in tuum
complexum. sed abit dies:
prodeas noua nupta.
o cubile, quod omnibus
* * * * * * *
* * * * * * *
* * * * * * *

candido pede lecti,
quae tuo ueniunt ero,
quanta gaudia, quae uaga
nocte, quae medio die
gaudeat! sed abit dies:

* * * * * *
* * * * * *
* * * * * *
* * * * * *

Her noble nature holds her back,
she weeps because she must go.
Cease your tears Aurunculeia,
there is nothing to fear.
There will never be a girl
more beautiful who will see
the light of day lift its
face from the ocean.
As the hyacinth flower
in a rich man's garden,
you stand above all others.
Come, step forward. The day
passes while you wait.
Come bride, it is time to
hear our words. See how the
torches flicker hair of gold
Come, step forward bride.
You will have a strong husband,
not given to callow acts
or shameful adulteries.
He will not want to lie
far from your soft breasts.
But as the living vine wraps
itself around a great elm,
so you shall embrace him. Come,
step forward young bride.
O marriage bed for all
* * * * * *
* * * * * *
* * * * * *

with ivory feet.

What joys wait for your
husband in the passing night
and in the heat of day.
Rejoice! Come forward bride.
O boys lift high the torches

prodeas noua nupta.
tollite, o pueri, faces:
flammeum uideo uenire.
ite concinite in modum
'io Hymen Hymenaee io,
io Hymen Hymenaee.'
ne diu taceat procax
Fescennina iocatio,
nec nuces pueris neget
desertum domini audiens
concubinus amorem.
da nuces pueris, iners
concubine! satis diu
lusisti nucibus: lubet
iam seruire Talasio.
concubine, nuces da.
sordebant tibi uillicae,
concubine, hodie atque heri:
nunc tuum cinerarius
tondet os. miser a miser
concubine, nuces da.
diceris male te a tuis
unguentate glabris marite
abstinere, sed abstine.
io Hymen Hymenaee io,
io Hymen Hymenaee.
scimus haec tibi quae licent
sola cognita, sed marito
ista non eadem licent.
io Hymen Hymenaee io,
io Hymen Hymenaee.
nupta, tu quoque quae tuus
uir petet caue ne neges,
ni petitum aliunde eat.
io Hymen Hymenaee io,
io Hymen Hymenaee.
en tibi domus ut potens
et beata uiri tui,
quae tibi sine seruiat
(io Hymen Hymenaee io,
io Hymen Hymenaee)

the bridal veil is approaching
Come, chant your chorus.
O Hymen, Hymenae,
O Hymen, Hymenae!
Crowd no longer hold back
your bawdy jokes.
He who was once a favourite
is now the subject of lewd
jokes. Yesterday's favourite,
a short time ago other men's
wives were not good enough
for you. Now you will have to
chase whatever you can catch.
Clean yourself up, shave off
your beard. You have played
with walnuts too much,
throw them away you must
serve another now. Some will
joke that when the scented
bridegroom has gone forth
he will have to be steered
away from any in his path.
Yet he will abstain.
O Hymen, hymenae,
O Hymen, hymenae!
Everyone knows you indulged
lawfully but for a married
man they are now forbidden
O Hymen, hymenae,
O Hymen, hymenae!
O bride never tease him,
then hold back your
beauty, always offer
him his sweet desire.
O Hymen, hymenae,
O Hymen, hymenae!
His blessed house powerful
and strong accepts you
now to join it.
O Hymen, hymenae,
O Hymen, hymenae!

usque dum tremulum mouens
cana tempus anilitas
omnia omnibus annuit.
io Hymen Hymenaee io,
io Hymen Hymenaee.
transfer omine cum bono
limen aureolos pedes,
rasilemque subi forem.
io Hymen Hymenaee io,
io Hymen Hymenaee.
aspice intus ut accubans
uir tuus Tyrio in toro
totus immineat tibi.
io Hymen Hymenaee io,
io Hymen Hymenaee.
illi non minus ac tibi
pectore uritur intimo
flamma, sed penite magis.
io Hymen Hymenaee io,
io Hymen Hymenaee.
mitte brachiolum teres,
praetextate, puellulae:
iam cubile adeat uiri.
io Hymen Hymenaee io,
io Hymen Hymenaee.
uos bonae senibus uiris
cognitae bene feminae,
collocate puellulam.
io Hymen Hymenaee io,
io Hymen Hymenaee.
iam licet uenias, marite:
uxor in thalamo tibi est,
ore floridulo nitens,
alba parthenice uelut
luteumue papauer.
at, marite, ita me iuuent
caelites, nihilo minus
pulcer es, neque te Venus
neglegit. sed abit dies:
perge, ne remorare.

Until your hair is grey
and age holds fast your
limbs may you say yes
to your marriage bond.
O Hymen. hymenae,
O Hymen. hymenae!
On golden feet pass
the threshold of good
omen disappearing through
the shining door.
O Hymen, hymenae,
O Hymen, hymenae!
Inside, your husband lies
stretching towards you,
his eyes burning with desire.
O Hymen, hymenae,
O Hymen, hymenae!
You are taunted by desire
but he is taunted far more
for the greatness of his
desire is hidden.
O Hymen, hymenae,
O Hymen, hymenae!
You boys who gently
hold her arms, let them go,
so she can now
greet her husband.
O Hymen, hymenae,
O Hymen, hymenae!
Honoured guests arise,
men of age and good women
escort her to her husband.
O Hymen, hymenae,
O Hymen, hymenae!
Husband your bride is beside
you now, her face is red as
poppies, her skin white as
daisies, she shines with
brightness. You are the same
in beauty. The heavens have
spared nothing in your creation

non diu remoratus es:
iam uenis. bona te Venus
iuuerit, quoniam palam
quod cupis cupis, et bonum
non abscondis amorem.
ille pulueris Africi
siderumque micantium
subducat numerum prius,
qui uestri numerare uolt
multa milia ludi.
ludite ut lubet, et breui
liberos date. non decet
tam uetus sine liberis
nomen esse, sed indidem
semper ingenerari.
Torquatus uolo paruulus
matris e gremio suae
porrigens teneras manus
dulce rideat ad patrem
semihiante labello.
sit suo similis patri
Manlio et facile insciis
noscitetur ab omnibus,
et pudicitiam suae
matris indicet ore.
talis illius a bona
matre laus genus approbet,
qualis unica ab optima
matre Telemacho manet
fama Penelopeo.
claudite ostia, uirgines:
lusimus satis. at boni
coniuges, bene uiuite et
munere assiduo ualentem
exercete iuuentam.

and Venus especially kind
towards you, still the day
passes. This is Venus's
jurisdiction. Her decree
is to let the husband
join with his wife.
Their marriage is complete.
What love can escape desire
like this? They should count
the stars in the sky and the
sands in the great desert,
those who want to know the
number of their bedroom kisses
before tomorrow's daylight
may they have made an heir
for so honoured a Roman house
and may that name never be lost.
Soon may a little torquatus
be held fast in his mother's
arms, reaching two little
hands to his dear father,
while a laugh comes from his
parted lips. May he so closely
resemble Manlius that all can see
his father's handsome frame,
telling also of his mother's
virtue. In action may this
son give his mother honour
as great as Telemachus
gave his mother Penelope.
The door must be closed
o virgins, our song must cease.
May they love well in their
youth and in their marriage
of old age and bring forth
a strong, noble generation.

LXIV.

PELIACO quondam prognatae uertice pinus
dicuntur liquidas Neptuni nasse per undas
Phasidos ad fluctus et fines Aeetaeos,
cum lecti iuuenes, Argiuae robora pubis,
auratam optantes Colchis auertere pellem
ausi sunt uada salsa cita decurrere puppi,
caerula uerrentes abiegnis aequora palmis.
diua quibus retinens in summis urbibus arces
ipsa leui fecit uolitantem flamine currum,
pinea coniungens inflexae texta carinae.
illa rudem cursu prima imbuit Amphitriten;
quae simul ac rostro uentosum proscidit aequor
tortaque remigio spumis incanuit unda,
emersere freti candenti e gurgite uultus
aequoreae monstrum Nereides admirantes.
illa, atque alia, uiderunt luce marinas
mortales oculis nudato corpore Nymphas
nutricum tenus exstantes e gurgite cano.
tum Thetidis Peleus incensus fertur amore,
tum Thetis humanos non despexit hymenaeos,
tum Thetidi pater ipse iugandum Pelea sensit.
o nimis optato saeclorum tempore nati
heroes, saluete, deum genus! o bona matrum
progenies, saluete iter...
uos ego saepe, meo uos carmine compellabo.
teque adeo eximie taedis felicibus aucte,
Thessaliae columen Peleu, cui Iuppiter ipse,
ipse suos diuum genitor concessit amores;
tene Thetis tenuit pulcerrima Nereine?
tene suam Tethys concessit ducere neptem,
Oceanusque, mari totum qui amplectitur orbem?
quae simul optatae finito tempore luces
aduenere, domum conuentu tota frequentat
Thessalia, oppletur laetanti regia coetu:
dona ferunt prae se, declarant gaudia uultu.
deseritur Cieros, linquunt Pthiotica Tempe
Crannonisque domos ac moenia Larisaea,
Pharsalum coeunt, Pharsalia tecta frequentant.

64.

On Pelion's height great trees were
transformed into ships to journey over
the waters passing through Neptune's
realm. Here King Aeetes' great land held
the golden fleece. The youthful heroes
of all of Greece dared to journey over
the salt sea with a fast ship, moving
oars as wings on the vast stretches of
blue. The goddess Pallas, protector
of cities and towns, made the ship
weaving the great hull and fashioning
her graceful keel. She then instructed
Amphitrite in the arts of sailing.
When the ship started cutting the water
with whiting foam, there arose from the
water the faces and naked breasts of
sea-nymphs marvelling at the ship's
form as she skimmed the surface.
Peleus then first saw Thetis in all
her beauty and she did not spurn
a mortal marriage. Her father
sanctioned the union with Peleus.
O heroes from a greater age,
o those sprung from the god,
those of great mothers,
may you be gracious to me.
I will turn to you often for
words. Peleus, great king of
Thessaly, was brought even more
esteem by his wedding to a goddess.
She, the most beautiful of the
sea-nymphs, Tethys nodded that
you should unite with her grandchild.
And Oceanus, whose seas circle
the World, gave his consent.
When that day came, all
Thessaly rejoiced and crowds

rura colit nemo, mollescunt colla iuuencis,
non humilis curuis purgatur uinea rastris,
non glebam prono conuellit uomere taurus,
non falx attenuat frondatorum arboris umbram,
squalida desertis rubigo infertur aratris.
ipsius at sedes, quacumque opulenta recessit
regia, fulgenti splendent auro atque argento.
candet ebur soliis, collucent pocula mensae,
tota domus gaudet regali splendida gaza.
puluinar uero diuae geniale locatur
sedibus in mediis, Indo quod dente politum
tincta tegit roseo conchyli purpura fuco.
haec uestis priscis hominum uariata figuris
heroum mira uirtutes indicat arte.
namque fluentisono prospectans litore Diae,
Thesea cedentem celeri cum classe tuetur
indomitos in corde gerens Ariadna furores,
necdum etiam sese quae uisit uisere credit,
utpote fallaci quae tum primum excita somno
desertam in sola miseram se cernat harena.
immemor at iuuenis fugiens pellit uada remis,
irrita uentosae linquens promissa procellae.
quem procul ex alga maestis Minois ocellis,
saxea ut effigies bacchantis, prospicit, eheu,
prospicit et magnis curarum fluctuat undis,
non flauo retinens subtilem uertice mitram,
non contecta leui uelatum pectus amictu,
non tereti strophio lactentis uincta papillas,
omnia quae toto delapsa e corpore passim
ipsius ante pedes fluctus salis alludebant.
sed neque tum mitrae neque tum fluitantis amictus
illa uicem curans toto ex te pectore, Theseu,
toto animo, tota pendebat perdita mente.
misera, assiduis quam luctibus externauit
spinosas Erycina serens in pectore curas,
illa tempestate, ferox quo ex tempore Theseus
egressus curuis e litoribus Piraei
attigit iniusti regis Gortynia templa.
nam perhibent olim crudeli peste coactam

celebrated in the city.
They carried flowers and
gifts into your halls.
The streets of Cieros were empty
and there was scarcely a soul in
any home. Tempe's groves were
silent, a great many of the people
were under the roof of Pharsaizia
to celebrate the marriage feast.
Cattle were alone in the fields,
the ripened vines were left untouched,
the oxen freed from the yoke,
and rust approached the plows.
Figures from more ancient
times were woven on the blanket.
Ariadne still stands on the shore
beyond the thundering surf
watching Theseus and his crew
sailing away from Naxos.
Her heart is torn with sorrow;
even in her abandonment she
still loves Theseus.
She was deceived by sleep,
waking to find herself alone
on the sand. He had set mast and
oar against the open sea, leaving
his promises. The princess looks
toward the sea still as a stone
Maenad. Her heart carries itself
across the distance unheard. A
bonnet has fallen from her long
hair, her princess' scarf and robe
are flung down beside her for the
tide to carry away. Her breasts
are naked and white. She doesn't
care if her clothes are carried away.
She is destroyed by love. Her heart
and soul hung on Theseus. Her gifts
of misery, whose thorns were to strike

Androgeoneae poenas exsoluere caedis
electos iuuenes simul et decus innuptarum
Cecropiam solitam esse dapem dare Minotauro.
quis angusta malis cum moenia uexarentur,
ipse suum Theseus pro caris corpus Athenis
proicere optauit potius quam talia Cretam
funera Cecropiae nec funera portarentur.
atque ita naue leui nitens ac lenibus auris
magnanimum ad Minoa uenit sedesque superbas.
hunc simul ac cupido conspexit lumine uirgo
regia, quam suauis exspirans castus odores
lectulus in molli complexu matris alebat,
quales Eurotae praecingunt flumina myrtus
auraue distinctos educit uerna colores,
non prius ex illo flagrantia declinauit
lumina, quam cuncto concepit corpore flammam
funditus atque imis exarsit tota medullis.
heu misere exagitans immiti corde furores
sancte puer, curis hominum qui gaudia misces,
quaeque regis Golgos quaeque Idalium frondosum,
qualibus incensam iactastis mente puellam
fluctibus, in flauo saepe hospite suspirantem!
quantos illa tulit languenti corde timores!
quanto saepe magis fulgore expalluit auri,
cum saeuum cupiens contra contendere monstrum
aut mortem appeteret Theseus aut praemia laudis!
non ingrata tamen frustra munuscula diuis
promittens tacito succepit uota labello.
nam uelut in summo quatientem brachia Tauro
quercum aut conigeram sudanti cortice pinum
indomitus turbo contorquens flamine robur,
eruit (illa procul radicitus exturbata
prona cadit, late quaeuis cumque obuia frangens,)
sic domito saeuum prostrauit corpore Theseus
nequiquam uanis iactantem cornua uentis.
inde pedem sospes multa cum laude reflexit
errabunda regens tenui uestigia filo,
ne labyrintheis e flexibus egredientem
tecti frustraretur inobseruabilis error.

again and again, were sealed when
brave Theseus left Piraus Harbour
toward the walls of the dark king
of Crete. It was to stop the great
plague that had fallen upon the city
from the murder of Androdgeos.
Young men and women were sent
each year in offering to the
Minotaur. Theseus then risked his
life for his long suffering Athens
and joined those who were to be
sent to Crete. In his friendship
he sped on favourable winds to those
strong walls. There he first met great
Minos, arrogant in his kingly power.
His daughter, raised by a sheltering
mother's care, secluded and perfumed,
was a royal virgin. She was as the
many-coloured flowers along the banks
of the river Eurotas where sweet myrtle
blooms with the breath of the coming
spring. She saw him for only a moment.
Her eyes were bright and a flame ran
through her. Unfortunate are those who
are struck by Cupid. They are made mad
with his joy and pain. And you who rule
futile Idalaium and Golgos, in what
depth of the sea did you lift to
drown her passion before setting
it back in her heart? Venus, you are
one of the least merciful gods.
Ariadne feared for the light-haired
foreigner. She trembled and her face
turned lighter than gold when she understood
Theseus' determination to win glory or
a noble death against the Minotaur.
Her breath between her lips was a living
prayer to the gods and they were pleased by
her promises. As a powerful wind on Itaurus
heaves great branches from the uppermost heights,

sed quid ego a primo digressus carmine plura
commemorem, ut linquens genitoris filia uultum,
ut consanguineae complexum, ut denique matris,
quae misera in gnata deperdita laeta
omnibus his Thesei dulcem praeoptarit amorem:
aut ut uecta rati spumosa ad litora Diae
aut ut eam deuinctam lumina somno
liquerit immemori discedens pectore coniunx?
saepe illam perhibent ardenti corde furentem
clarisonas imo fudisse e pectore uoces,
ac tum praeruptos tristem conscendere montes,
unde aciem pelagi uastos protenderet aestus,
tum tremuli salis aduersas procurrere in undas
mollia nudatae tollentem tegmina surae,
atque haec extremis maestam dixisse querellis,
frigidulos udo singultus ore cientem:
'sicine me patriis auectam, perfide, ab aris
perfide, deserto liquisti in litore, Theseu?
sicine discedens neglecto numine diuum,
immemor a! deuota domum periuria portas?
nullane res potuit crudelis flectere mentis
consilium? tibi nulla fuit clementia praesto,
immite ut nostri uellet miserescere pectus?
at non haec quondam blanda promissa dedisti
uoce mihi, non haec miserae sperare iubebas,
sed conubia laeta, sed optatos hymenaeos,
quae cuncta aereii discerpunt irrita uenti.
nunc iam nulla uiro iuranti femina credat,
nulla uiri speret sermones esse fideles;
quis dum aliquid cupiens animus praegestit apisci,
nil metuunt iurare, nihil promittere parcunt:
sed simul ac cupidae mentis satiata libido est,
dicta nihil metuere, nihil periuria curant.
certe ego te in medio uersantem turbine leti
eripui, et potius germanum amittere creui,
quam tibi fallaci supremo in tempore dessem.
pro quo dilaceranda feris dabor alitibusque
praeda, neque iniacta tumulabor mortua terra.

before a mighty gust upends a great oak
or lofty pine and sends it crashing to
the earth its roots broken and lifted
into the air, its bulk sprawled along the
ground, so Theseus overthrew the great bull
who lay bleeding and stabbing the empty
air with his horns. Safely he retraced his
steps using the string she had given him,
through the confusing labyrinth turning
corner after corner, grateful at every step
for the thread she had given him to overcome
his confusion. But why do I digress?
Why should I sing of a princess
looking away from her father's eyes
and the love of a mother and the affection
of a loving sister? Unfortunate one who
chose Theseus above them all. And he took
her in his great ship to foam-sprayed
Naxos. There sleep clasped her in his
arms and spoke into her eyes until
she was lost in her husband's arms.
Then Theseus left her there on the sand.
It is well known that she woke overcome
with grief and the depth of her sorrowful
cries moved the stones to pity. In her fright,
she ran to the highest vantage point,
her eyes scanned the great width of the sea.
Then she ran back to the shore and ran into
the oncoming waves toward his distant ship.
Finally through her exhaustion and tears
in the depth of unhappiness she cried aloud:
"You betrayed me, was there no pity in your
heart for me? You took me from my family
altars, from my loved ones and my home,
to leave me on this rocky shore. Far more
than hurting me, you have offended the gods.
In your ship you carry ravaged promises.
Hero, would you stop at nothing to achieve
your end? Did you ever find a scrap of pity
for me in your hardened heart? With a gentle
voice you gave me a joyful oath of love.

Catullus

91

quaenam te genuit sola sub rupe leaena,
quod mare conceptum spumantibus exspuit undis,
quae Syrtis, quae Scylla rapax, quae uasta Carybdis,
talia qui reddis pro dulci praemia uita?
si tibi non cordi fuerant conubia nostra,
saeua quod horrebas prisci praecepta parentis,
attamen in uestras potuisti ducere sedes,
quae tibi iucundo famularer serua labore,
candida permulcens liquidis uestigia lymphis,
purpureaue tuum consternens ueste cubile.
sed quid ego ignaris nequiquam conquerar auris,
externata malo, quae nullis sensibus auctae
nec missas audire queunt nec reddere uoces?
ille autem prope iam mediis uersatur in undis,
nec quisquam apparet uacua mortalis in alga.
sic nimis insultans extremo tempore saeua
fors etiam nostris inuidit questibus auris.
Iuppiter omnipotens, utinam ne tempore primo
Gnosia Cecropiae tetigissent litora puppes,
indomito nec dira ferens stipendia tauro
perfidus in Cretam religasset nauita funem,
nec malus hic celans dulci crudelia forma
consilia in nostris requiesset sedibus hospes!
nam quo me referam? quali spe perdita nitor?
Idaeosne petam montes? at gurgite lato
discernens ponti truculentum diuidit aequor.
an patris auxilium sperem? quemne ipsa reliqui
respersum iuuenem fraterna caede secuta?
coniugis an fido consoler memet amore?
quine fugit lentos incuruans gurgite remos?
praeterea nullo colitur sola insula tecto,
nec patet egressus pelagi cingentibus undis.
nulla fugae ratio, nulla spes: omnia muta,
omnia sunt deserta, ostentant omnia letum.
non tamen ante mihi languescent lumina morte,
nec prius a fesso secedent corpore sensus,
quam iustam a diuis ecam prodita multam
caelestumque fidem postrema comprecer hora.
quare facta uirum multantes uindice poena

I thought I would be your wife and a queen.
My words are beaten away and lost by the
strong wind. When men are lustful they are
full of promises, but once Cupid has fulfilled
their desire, they have no memory of their speeches.
No woman should believe them. Theseus, when death
spirits were hovering around you and breathed at
the corners of your face, I alone saved you from
their grasp. I chose you over my brother. Now I
shall lie naked and unburied on this shore.
Carrion birds will feast on my corpse which is
a sin against the gods. What harsh lioness bore
you in a rocky crag? What sea vomited you up
from its spume? The quicksands of Africa,
Charybdis' terrible flow, or the many-headed
monster Scylla, eater of human flesh?
This is what you give me for your life?
If you had some fear in marrying me
because I am not from your county
and that your father would not approve,
I would have rather been your slave.
I would have been glad to wash your feet in
your halls and set the purple coverlets on your
chairs and beds. But I cry to the unknowing wind
that is deaf and has no voice. Nearing his home,
he senses a triumphant return while I am in a
forsaken place with my memory tormenting me and
not people but seaweed covering its shores.
Great Jupiter, if only the great ships were
lost at sea or never reached upon Cretan shores
misery would never have been speaking with
my mouth. And their receiving hero would
never have killed the great bull.
Was his graceful speech and manner
a mask for a truly heartless man?
All hope has fled from me and I have nowhere
to flee. The great sea cuts me off from my home.
My father would not help me now. I brought about
the destruction of my brother and I, myself, too.
Theseus is heaving hard and his men are heaving hard

Catullus

93

Eumenides, quibus anguino redimita capillo
frons exspirantis praeportat pectoris iras,
huc huc aduentate, meas audite querellas,
quas ego, uae misera, extremis proferre medullis
cogor inops, ardens, amenti caeca furore.
quae quoniam uerae nascuntur pectore ab imo,
uos nolite pati nostrum uanescere luctum,
sed quali solam Theseus me mente reliquit,
tali mente, deae, funestet seque suosque.'
has postquam maesto profudit pectore uoces,
supplicium saeuis ecens anxia factis,
annuit inuicto caelestum numine rector;
quo motu tellus atque horrida contremuerunt
aequora concussitque micantia sidera mundus.
ipse autem caeca mentem caligine Theseus
consitus oblito dimisit pectore cuncta,
quae mandata prius constanti mente tenebat,
dulcia nec maesto sustollens signa parenti
sospitem Erechtheum se ostendit uisere portum.
namque ferunt olim, classi cum moenia diuae
linquentem gnatum uentis concrederet Aegeus,
talia complexum iuueni mandata dedisse:
'gnate mihi longa iucundior unice uita,
gnate, ego quem in dubios cogor dimittere casus,
reddite in extrema nuper mihi fine senectae,
quandoquidem fortuna mea ac tua feruida uirtus
eripit inuito mihi te, cui languida nondum
lumina sunt gnati cara saturata figura,
non ego te gaudens laetanti pectore mittam,
nec te ferre sinam fortunae signa secundae,
sed primum multas expromam mente querellas,
canitiem terra atque infuso puluere foedans,
inde infecta uago suspendam lintea malo,
nostros ut luctus nostraeque incendia mentis
carbasus obscurata dicet ferrugine Hibera.
quod tibi si sancti concesserit incola Itoni,
quae nostrum genus ac sedes defendere Erecthei
annuit, ut tauri respergas sanguine dextram,
tum uero facito ut memori tibi condita corde

at their oars under an open sail to free himself
from me. I thought he was to be my husband.
I feel madness approaching me.
I can see no house on this desolate island.
I am to languish before the very light of death,
I am held here by the sea to the solitude of my
own voice. I shall use it to ask retribution of
the gods for such a betrayal. O you Furies!
Avenging spirits who punish the human acts of sin.
Your hair breathes living snakes. Bring forth
your storms from your bloodless hearts.
Milk your rage that seethes there. Hear the words
of my love-deceived mind. O Goddesses make my
execration strong and weigh as heavily on him
as his cruelty weighs on me. Let Theseus meet
as wretched an end as befell me. After her
voice silenced, the great master of the
depths nodded his head. The stars in the
heavens shook. The sea rolled and the earth
heaved with a sigh. A gentle cloud came over
Theseus when he was in sight of land. He did not
remember to lift the white sail on his ship
and as his ship drew close his father saw no
favourable sign. It is said that when Aegeus's
son was given away from Athena's towers
the king's parting words were these:
"More dear to me than long life,
my son who has only recently come back
to me at the end of my days, now I have
to send you far away from my sight
on a dangerous voyage. Such is my
fortune. Your courage pulls you away
from my failing eyes before they have
drunk their contentment of your face.
My son, neither with joy or with a light heart
do I watch you lift Iberian sail and mast.
I am torn with sorrow and my imagination wanders
in its agony. I soil my grey head with the earth
and the sand at my feet. If the goddess of Itonus'
sacred shrine, a sworn defender of the city and

haec uigeant mandata, nec ulla oblitteret aetas;
ut simul ac nostros inuisent lumina collis,
funestam antennae deponant undique uestem,
candidaque intorti sustollant uela rudentes,
quam primum cernens ut laeta gaudia mente
agnoscam, cum te reducem aetas prospera sistet.'
haec mandata prius constanti mente tenentem
Thesea ceu pulsae uentorum flamine nubes
aereum niuei montis liquere cacumen.
at pater, ut summa prospectum ex arce petebat,
anxia in assiduos absumens lumina fletus,
cum primum infecti conspexit lintea ueli,
praecipitem sese scopulorum e uertice iecit,
amissum credens immiti Thesea fato.
sic funesta domus ingressus tecta paterna
morte ferox Theseus, qualem Minoidi luctum
obtulerat mente immemori, talem ipse recepit.
quae tum prospectans cedentem maesta carinam
multiplices animo uoluebat saucia curas.
at parte ex alia florens uolitabat Iacchus
cum thiaso Satyrorum et Nysigenis Silenis,
te quaerens, Ariadna, tuoque incensus amore.
* * * * * * * *

quae tum alacres passim lymphata mente furebant
euhoe bacchantes, euhoe capita inflectentes.
harum pars tecta quatiebant cuspide thyrsos,
pars e diuolso iactabant membra iuuenco,
pars sese tortis serpentibus incingebant,
pars obscura cauis celebrabant orgia cistis,
orgia quae frustra cupiunt audire profani;
plangebant aliae proceris tympana palmis,
aut tereti tenuis tinnitus aere ciebant;
multis raucisonos efflabant cornua bombos
barbaraque horribili stridebat tibia cantu.
talibus amplifice uestis decorata figuris
puluinar complexa suo uelabat amictu.
quae postquam cupide spectando Thessala pubes
expleta est, sanctis coepit decedere diuis.
hic, qualis flatu placidum mare matutino

its people, allows your right hand to be soaked
in the blood of the bull sacrifice, hold these words
in your memory and in your heart that they may not
be forgotten. Upon your return, as soon as your eyes
come across the tops of our hills, before the land
is even a solid mass, put away your black sails
and lift the lesser white sails so it will sooner
quell the dread in my heart at your approach.
By that I will know that you are safe.
Your proud return will be a joy to me and the
city." Clouds from the snow-capped mountains
were blown by the wind over the land
carrying Theseus' ship out to sea.
With these words sealed in his mind
his father, the king, returned to his palace
and waited in fear for the day of Theseus'
return. On that day when he first saw the ship
and its black sails, he thought all had been lost.
His weeping was without cease until he hurled
himself off the top of the cliffs above the city.
In such a way, did Theseus enter his father's house,
having sorrow greet him at his father's doorstep.
Ariadne in her sorrow watched the ship disappear
over the water. On another part of the quilt
Bacchus, in the full flush of youth,
accompanied by his attendants
and satyrs from Mount Nysa, is searching
for you Ariadne and desires your love.
* * * * * * *

Suddenly present around you, the maenads
are dancing in a frenzied circle crying out
"Euohe! Euohe!" their heads thrown back, their
faces toward the sky. Some were carrying sacred
thyrses and spears, others were throwing about
dismembered limbs of a bull. Some were
draped with twining serpents, some were
solemnly carrying caskets full of things
only known to the Mysteries and which
the uninitiated always want to learn.

horrificans Zephyrus procliuas incitat undas,
Aurora exoriente uagi sub limina Solis,
quae tarde primum clementi flamine pulsae
procedunt leuiterque sonant plangore cachinni,
post uento crescente magis magis increbescunt,
purpureaque procul nantes ab luce refulgent:
sic tum uestibuli linquentes regia tecta
ad se quisque uago passim pede discedebant.
quorum post abitum princeps e uertice Pelei
aduenit Chiron portans siluestria dona:
nam quoscumque ferunt campi, quos Thessala magnis
montibus ora creat, quos propter fluminis undas
aura parit flores tepidi fecunda Fauoni,
hos indistinctis plexos tulit ipse corollis,
quo permulsa domus iucundo risit odore.
confestim Penios adest, uiridantia Tempe,
Tempe, quae siluae cingunt super impendentes,
Minosim linquens doris celebranda choreis,
non uacuos: namque ille tulit radicitus altas
fagos ac recto proceras stipite laurus,
non sine nutanti platano lentaque sorore
flammati Phaethontis et aerea cupressu.
haec circum sedes late contexta locauit,
uestibulum ut molli uelatum fronde uireret.
post hunc consequitur sollerti corde Prometheus,
extenuata gerens ueteris uestigia poenae,
quam quondam silici restrictus membra catena
persoluit pendens e uerticibus praeruptis.
inde pater diuum sancta cum coniuge natisque
aduenit caelo, te solum, Phoebe, relinquens
unigenamque simul cultricem montibus Idri:
Pelea nam tecum pariter soror aspernata est,
nec Thetidis taedas uoluit celebrare iugales.
qui postquam niueis flexerunt sedibus artus
large multiplici constructae sunt dape mensae,
cum interea infirmo quatientes corpora motu
ueridicos Parcae coeperunt edere cantus.
his corpus tremulum complectens undique uestis
candida purpurea talos incinxerat ora,

Some were beating shallow drums and
tambourines to strange rhythms.
Through the harsh sounds of horns,
and polished bronze objects, a flute
makes eerie sounds. These were the
figures, beautifully woven on the
coverlet. When the young Thessalians'
eyes were filled with these magnificent
and graceful works, they moved aside waiting
for the immortal gods. They parted as
the morning breath of the west wind
brings forth waves for the rising dawn,
before she stretches herself into the
horizon, before the arrival of the sun.
The waves come forth with a quiet laughter
gently at first, then following stronger
winds as there becomes more light.
With steady feet, each guest leaves the
forecourt of the palace. Chiron was the
first to appear coming from Mount Peleus.
He brought gifts from Thessaly, gifts
from the forest and from the flowery fields
of the land. He brought every kind of
flower that the warm winds help to nurse
by the rivers between the rough mountains.
He carried them himself also bearing small
wreaths. The house laughed and was pleased by
their sweet fragrance. After, Peneus came from
the valley of Tempe, which is covered by thick
forests. He bought great beech trees, and
high laurels with straight trunks, tall
Cypresses and bay trees and Poplars, which
are sisters of Phaethon who carries the sun.
He placed these gifts around the palace of Peleus
and made the forecourt thick with leafy foliage.
After, the inventive Prometheus came, still showing
the scars of his ancient punishment that he once
suffered when he was chained on the Scythian heights.
The father of the gods came next with his lovely

at roseae niueo residebant uertice uittae,
aeternumque manus carpebant rite laborem.
laeua colum molli lana retinebat amictum,
dextera tum leuiter deducens fila supinis
formabat digitis, tum prono in pollice torquens
libratum tereti uersabat turbine fusum,
atque ita decerpens aequabat semper opus dens,
laneaque aridulis haerebant morsa labellis,
quae prius in leui fuerant exstantia filo:
ante pedes autem candentis mollia lanae
uellera uirgati custodibant calathisci.
haec tum clarisona pellentes uellera uoce
talia diuino fuderunt carmine fata,
carmine, perfidiae quod post nulla arguet aetas.
o decus eximium magnis uirtutibus augens,
Emathiae tutamen, Opis carissime nato,
accipe, quod laeta tibi pandunt luce sorores,
ueridicum oraclum: sed uos, quae fata sequuntur,
currite ducentes subtegmina, currite, fusi.
adueniet tibi iam portans optata maritis
Hesperus, adueniet fausto cum sidere coniunx,
quae tibi flexanimo mentem perfundat amore,
languidulosque paret tecum coniungere somnos,
leuia substernens robusto bracchia collo.
currite ducentes subtegmina, currite, fusi.
nulla domus tales umquam contexit amores,
nullus amor tali coniunxit foedere amantes,
qualis adest Thetidi, qualis concordia Peleo.
currite ducentes subtegmina, currite, fusi.
nascetur uobis expers terroris Achilles,
hostibus haud tergo, sed forti pectore notus,
qui persaepe uago uictor certamine cursus
flammea praeuertet celeris uestigia ceruae.
currite ducentes subtegmina, currite, fusi.
non illi quisquam bello se conferet heros,
cum Phrygii Teucro manabunt sanguine
Troicaque obsidens longinquo moenia bello,
periuri Pelopis uastabit tertius heres.

queen and children. Only Phoebus, Apollo and his
twin sister goddess of the mountains and forest
of Idrus were absent. She, like you Apollo, disdained
Peleus and would not grant honour to the wedding
feast by her presence. The gods were seated on ivory
chairs, the tables were piled high with delicacies.
It was then that the trembling fates,
their bodies wrapped in white cloaks fringed
in purple, with purple at their feet
and red bands around their white hair, came.
Their hands continuing their eternal work,
the distaff wrapped in wool, held in the left
hand with wool gently pulled over by the right
hand's upturned fingers, shaping thread turning
their spindles with their thumb turned toward
the ground. They clean the wool with their teeth,
the excess wool clinging to their dry lips
slowly filling osier baskets at their feet.
During this, their hollow voices spoke
inexorable prophecies unfailing in their truth:
'O Peleus, your great virtue augments your honour.
Guardian of Amathia, favoured of Jupiter,
hear your sisters' words revealed to you
by the light of day, a truthful oracle.

Run spindles weave your fate. Run.

The evening star will come soon
and carry the bridegroom to his desire.
The light of wedding torches will lead the way.
Peleus your heart is overcome with desire for
her soft arms to be clasped around you,
touching your strong neck.

Run spindles weave your fate. Run.

No home has ever
held lovers so greatly bound to each
other. Such is the great harmony
for Thetis and Peleus.

currite ducentes subtegmina, currite, fusi.
illius egregias uirtutes claraque facta
saepe fatebuntur gnatorum in funere matres,
cum incultum cano soluent a uertice crinem,
putridaque infirmis uariabunt pectora palmis.
currite ducentes subtegmina, currite, fusi.
namque uelut densas praecerpens messor aristas
sole sub ardenti flauentia demetit arua,
Troiugenum infesto prosternet corpora ferro.
currite ducentes subtegmina, currite, fusi.
testis erit magnis uirtutibus unda Scamandri,
quae passim rapido diffunditur Hellesponto,
cuius iter caesis angustans corporum aceruis
alta tepefaciet permixta flumina caede.
currite ducentes subtegmina, currite, fusi.
adueniet tibi iam portans optata maritis
Hesperus, adueniet fausto cum sidere coniunx,
quae tibi flexanimo mentem perfundat amore,
languidulosque paret tecum coniungere somnos,
leuia substernens robusto bracchia collo.
currite ducentes subtegmina, currite, fusi.
nulla domus tales umquam contexit amores,
nullus amor tali coniunxit foedere amantes,
qualis adest Thetidi, qualis concordia Peleo.
currite ducentes subtegmina, currite, fusi.
nascetur uobis expers terroris Achilles,
hostibus haud tergo, sed forti pectore notus,
qui persaepe uago uictor certamine cursus
flammea praeuertet celeris uestigia ceruae.
currite ducentes subtegmina, currite, fusi.
non illi quisquam bello se conferet heros,
cum Phrygii Teucro manabunt sanguine
Troicaque obsidens longinquo moenia bello,
periuri Pelopis uastabit tertius heres.
currite ducentes subtegmina, currite, fusi.
illius egregias uirtutes claraque facta
saepe fatebuntur gnatorum in funere matres,
cum incultum cano soluent a uertice crinem,
putridaque infirmis uariabunt pectora palmis.

Run spindles weave your fate. Run.

Achilles will be
born to you. He will be unknown to fear.
His enemies will not know him by his
back. They will know only his great
chest. He will have great speed,
which often turns the tide of
battle running down his foes,
even to the speed of a deer.

Run spindles weave your fate. Run.

When the plains of Troy run red
with the blood of Trojan men,
there will be no Trojan willing
to fight him before the third heir
of Pelops breaks through the walls.

Run spindles weave your fate. Run.
When they recount his glorious deeds
at the graves of their sons.

Run spindles weave your fate run

As the farmer at the time of harvest
cuts down wheat with his scythe,
so Achilles will cut down a great number
of the warriors of Troy. And their
bodies will lie in the sun.

Run spindles weave your fate. Run.

Scamander will be filled with the
corpses of Achilles' work, bringing
great sorrow to the Trojans.
The river will run red and
its depth will be warmed
by the blood slowing its course
to the great Hellespont.

currite ducentes subtegmina, currite, fusi.
namque uelut densas praecerpens messor aristas
sole sub ardenti flauentia demetit arua,
Troiugenum infesto prosternet corpora ferro.
currite ducentes subtegmina, currite, fusi.
testis erit magnis uirtutibus unda Scamandri,
quae passim rapido diffunditur Hellesponto,
cuius iter caesis angustans corporum aceruis
alta tepefaciet permixta flumina caede.
currite ducentes subtegmina, currite, fusi.
denique testis erit morti quoque reddita praeda,
cum teres excelso coaceruatum aggere bustum
excipiet niueos perculsae uirginis artus.
currite ducentes subtegmina, currite, fusi.
nam simul ac fessis dederit fors copiam Achiuis
urbis Dardaniae Neptunia soluere uincla,
alta Polyxenia madefient caede sepulcra;
quae, uelut ancipiti succumbens uictima ferro,
proiciet truncum summisso poplite corpus.
currite ducentes subtegmina, currite, fusi.
quare agite optatos animi coniungite amores.
accipiat coniunx felici foedere diuam,
dedatur cupido iam dudum nupta marito.
currite ducentes subtegmina, currite, fusi.
non illam nutrix orienti luce reuisens
hesterno collum poterit circumdare filo,
anxia nec mater discordis maesta puellae
secubitu caros mittet sperare nepotes.
currite ducentes subtegmina, currite, fusi.
talia praefantes quondam felicia Pelei
carmina diuino cecinerunt pectore Parcae.
praesentes namque ante domos inuisere castas
heroum, et sese mortali ostendere coetu,
caelicolae nondum spreta pietate solebant.
saepe pater diuum templo in fulgente reuisens,
annua cum festis uenissent sacra diebus,
conspexit terra centum procumbere tauros.
saepe uagus Liber Parnasi uertice summo
Thyiadas effusis euantis crinibus egit,
cum Delphi tota certatim ex urbe ruentes

Run spindles weave your fate. Run.

O captive daughter of Priam, on
a great pyre you will clasp your
snowy arms to death.

Run spindles weave your fate. Run.

After Fortuna will show the war-torn Greeks
how to get past the walls that Neptune built,
Polyxenas' blood will run from the sacrificial
axe her headless body falling from Janus' blade.

Run spindles weave your fate. Run.

Join together in the delights of love,
let Peleus and Thetis be joined in a joyful
oath and give the bride to her eager husband.

She has changed!
Thetis' nurse arriving at dawn
will not be able to fit
the necklace around her neck
that fit the day before.

Run spindles weave your fate. Run.

The anxious mother
need not fear she will lack
for grandchildren
because of a quarrelsome daughter.

Run spindles weave your fate. Run.

Such songs were sung by the divine
fates of Peleus' future. In mortal
disguise when they used to visit
the dwellings of heroes, before
their righteous worship
was scorned on festal days,

acciperent laeti diuum fumantibus aris.
saepe in letifero belli certamine Mauors
aut rapidi Tritonis era aut Amarunsia uirgo
armatas hominum est praesens hortata cateruas.
sed postquam tellus scelere est imbuta nefando
iustitiamque omnes cupida de mente fugarunt,
perfudere manus fraterno sanguine fratres,
destitit extinctos gnatus lugere parentes,
optauit genitor primaeui funera nati,
liber ut innuptae poteretur flore nouercae,
ignaro mater substernens se impia nato
impia non uerita est diuos scelerare penates.
omnia fanda nefanda malo permixta furore
iustificam nobis mentem auertere deorum.
quare nec talis dignantur uisere coetus,
nec se contingi patiuntur lumine claro.

did the father of the gods
look out from his temple on
the sacrifice of a hundred bulls
as they fell to the earth.
Often wandering on the
highest summit of Parnassus,
Bacchus led his throng of Maenads
with loosened hair shouting 'Euhoe!'
as Delphi offered up to him
great burning offerings
and welcomed with joy his arrival.
Often in mortal combat did Mars
urge on combatants or Athena,
protector of Triton's river, or
Artemis of the hunt spur them on
to valour. But after the earth
was exposed by men to heinous
crime and justice was spurned,
men bathed their hands.

Run spindles weave your fate run
in their brother's blood.
Sons did not grieve at the death
of their parents; fathers yearned
for their sons' deaths so they could
enjoy the consorts of their sons;
and mothers offered themselves
to their unknowing sons, offending
the household gods. These offences,
even if sanctioned by human law,
have turned the gods away from
us. The just gods no longer attend
human assemblies or allow themselves
to be seen by the light of day.

LXV.

ETSI me assiduo confectum cura dolore
seuocat a doctis, Ortale, uirginibus,
nec potis est dulcis Musarum expromere fetus
mens animi, tantis fluctuat ipsa malis—
namque mei nuper Lethaeo in gurgite fratris
pallidulum manans alluit unda pedem,
Troia Rhoeteo quem subter litore tellus
ereptum nostris obterit ex oculis.
* * * * * * * *
numquam ego te, uita frater amabilior,
aspiciam posthac? at certe semper amabo,
semper maesta tua carmina morte canam,
qualia sub densis ramorum concinit umbris
Daulias, absumpti fata gemens Ityli—
sed tamen in tantis maeroribus, Ortale, mitto
haec expressa tibi carmina Battiadae,
ne tua dicta uagis nequiquam credita uentis
effluxisse meo forte putes animo,
ut missum sponsi furtiuo munere malum
procurrit casto uirginis e gremio,
quod miserae oblitae molli sub ueste locatum,
dum aduentu matris prosilit, excutitur,
atque illud prono praeceps agitur decursu,
huic manat tristi conscius ore rubor.

65.

Hortalus, I am torn by grief and my
heart is heavy from incessant sorrow.
The graceful Muses' births are far away
from me, my mind and my soul waver greatly.
Only a short time ago one of Lethe's waves
gently touched the pale foot of my brother,
taking him forever from my sight.
He is now under the shore of
Rhoteum clothed in Trojan ground.
****

My brother, more dear to me than life,
never again will my eyes see you.
The sorrow of your death never will
be far from me. It will linger
in my song as the nightingale hidden
in branches and shadow calls out
in sorrow for Itylus to come to
her side. But even in my despair
Hortalus, I send you now some
translations from Calimachus so
you will know that I still hold
you in my heart. Your words were
not forgotten and scattered on
the winds, as a young girl who
is startled moves suddenly,
forgetting the apple on her lap,
spoiling the gift from her young lover.

LXIX.

NOLI admirari, quare tibi femina nulla,
Rufe, uelit tenerum supposuisse femur,
non si illam rarae labefactes munere uestis
aut perluciduli deliciis lapidis.
laedit te quaedam mala fabula, qua tibi fertur
ualle sub alarum trux habitare caper.
hunc metuunt omnes, neque mirum: nam mala ualde est
bestia, nec quicum bella puella cubet.
quare aut crudelem nasorum interfice pestem,
aut admirari desine cur fugiunt.

69.

How can you be so surprised
no woman will embrace you Rufus;
even when you tempt their virtue
with rare gifts and beautiful
clothes, even when you give
them valuable stones, they
shrink from your naked embrace.
The reason is that you smell like
a goat, and when you lift your arms
you smell like the whole herd. But
you are so used to it, you can no
longer smell it. So get rid of
your beast and stop asking why the
women of Rome have such high virtue.

LXX.

NVLLI se dicit mulier mea nubere malle
quam mihi, non si se Iuppiter ipse petat.
dicit: sed mulier cupido quod dicit amanti,
in uento et rapida scribere oportet aqua.

70.

She swears she would not
take even Jupiter before me
if he came asking for her hand,
but what a woman promises to her
lover might as well be written
on the wind or in the raging Tiber.

LXXI.

SI cui iure bono sacer alarum obstitit hircus,
aut si quem merito tarda podagra secat.
aemulus iste tuus, qui uestrem exercet amorem,
mirifice est a te nactus utrumque malum.
nam quotiens futuit, totiens ulciscitur ambos:
illam affligit odore, ipse perit podagra.

71.

He is half-crippled with arthritis and
can hardly get hard enough to service her.
She is made sick by the putrid odour from his
armpits. You can consider yourself avenged my
friend. In bed at night, while he is stinking
and in pain, she must miss you. And more joy:
they say he has inherited all of your diseases.

LXXIII.

DESINE de quoquam quicquam bene uelle mereri
aut aliquem fieri posse putare pium.
omnia sunt ingrata, nihil fecisse benigne
immo etiam taedet obestque magis;
ut mihi, quem nemo grauius nec acerbius urget,
quam modo qui me unum atque unicum amicum habuit.

73.

Never expect kindness returned
or courtesy to be met by a grateful
heart. Few honour the gods.
The ingrate world is hearty and
strong. The well-meaning act is met
with suspicion and you may find
yourself open to a hostile act.
Even your best friend, if you are
not careful, can become your enemy.

LXXIV.

GELLIVS audierat patruum obiurgare solere,
si quis delicias diceret aut faceret.
hoc ne ipsi accideret, patrui perdepsuit ipsam
uxorem, et patruum reddidit Arpocratem.
quod uoluit fecit: nam, quamuis irrumet ipsum
nunc patruum, uerbum non faciet patruus.

74.

Gellius kept hearing his uncle lecturing
anyone who ever talked about love.
To shut him up, he debauched his uncle's
wife. His uncle was struck dumb
and can't seem to utter a word,
even if Gellius talks about boning him.

LXXV.

HVC est mens deducta tua mea, Lesbia, culpa
atque ita se officio perdidit ipsa suo,
ut iam nec bene uelle queat tibi, si optima fias,
nec desistere amare, omnia si facias.

75.

Lesbia, you are the author of my destruction.
My heart is defeated and weary at the thought of life.
I will wish terrible things for you if you become great,
but I will always love you just the same.

LXXIX.

LESBIVS est pulcer. quid ni? quem Lesbia malit
quam te cum tota gente, Catulle, tua.
sed tamen hic pulcer uendat cum gente Catullum,
si tria natorum suauia reppererit.

79.

Lesbia's new lover is beautiful
because he has an ancient name.
And this beautiful man can sell
Catullus and his whole family
if he can find even three of
the grossest street whores who
enjoy kissing his slobbering face.

LXXXIII.

LESBIA mi praesente uiro mala plurima dicit:
haec illi fatuo maxima laetitia est.
mule, nihil sentis? si nostri oblita taceret,
sana esset: nunc quod gannit et obloquitur,
non solum meminit, sed, quae multo acrior est res,
irata est. hoc est, uritur et loquitur.

83.

Lesbia, in the presence of her
husband, hurls abuse on my head.
The silly mule finds it entertaining.
If she felt nothing, she would be
silent and turn away, but her barks
and growls prove she too remembers,
and that memory drives her wagging tongue.

LXXXV.

ODI et amo. quare id faciam, fortasse requiris.
nescio, sed fieri sentio et excrucior.

85.

I hate and love. If you ask me why,
I do not know. But I feel tormented.

LXXXVII.

NVLLA potest mulier tantum se dicere amatam
uere, quantum a me Lesbia amata mea est.
nulla fides ullo fuit umquam foedere tanta,
quanta in amore tuo ex parte reperta mea est.

87.

Lesbia, no woman
can ever say truthfully,
that she has been loved
by any man as much as
I have loved you.
And no man has ever
been more faithful
in his pledge of love
than I have been to you.

LXXXVIII.

QVID facit is, Gelli, qui cum matre atque sorore
prurit, et abiectis peruigilat tunicis?
quid facit is, patruum qui non sinit esse maritum?
ecquid scis quantum suscipiat sceleris?
suscipit, o Gelli, quantum non ultima Tethys
nec genitor Nympharum abluit Oceanus:
nam nihil est quicquam sceleris, quo prodeat ultra,
non si demisso se ipse uoret capite.

88.

Gellius, what are you doing
staying up all night with
your mother and sister
in their underwear and
then entirely undressed?
You are making a
cuckold of your uncle.
O Gellius, don't you
know the hole you are
digging for yourself! The
gods will remember. Tethys,
mother of rivers, can never
wash you clean. Her husband,
the great Ocean, can't even
do it, you are so foul. If
you were an acrobat, you would
no doubt be putting your head
between your legs and swallowing.

LXXXIX.

GELLIVS est tenuis: quid ni? cui tam bona mater
tamque ualens uiuat tamque uenusta soror
tamque bonus patruus tamque omnia plena puellis
cognatis, quare is desinat esse macer?
qui ut nihil attingat, nisi quod fas tangere non est,
quantumuis quare sit macer inuenies.

89.

Gellius is thin, why would he not be?
His mother and beautiful sister never
cease doting on him; his uncle spares
him no expense; he has many attractive
girl cousins. With so many wanting to
please him, how could he not be skinny?
With the slightest knowledge of his tastes,
it's clear why he is as thin as a snake.

XC.

NASCATVR magus ex Gelli matrisque nefando
coniugio et discat Persicum aruspicium:
nam magus ex matre et gnato gignatur oportet,
si uera est Persarum impia religio,
gratus ut accepto ueneretur carmine diuos
omentum in flamma pingue liquefaciens.

90.

Let there be born a magus from Gellius's
unholy coupling with his mother
and let him grow up to learn the
arts of Persian divination. For they
actually believe that such a brat
should be highly revered and be let
to pick the entrails at the sacrifice
and howl out religious sounding things
while the crowd swoons in its disgrace.

XCIII.

NIL nimium studeo, Caesar, tibi uelle placere,
nec scire utrum sis albus an ater homo.

93.

Caesar, you, your nasty
habits and your appearance
have no interest for me.

XCVI.

SI quicquam mutis gratum acceptumque sepulcris
accidere a nostro, Calue, dolore potest,
quo desiderio ueteres renouamus amores
atque olim missas flemus amicitias,
certe non tanto mors immatura dolori est
Quintiliae, quantum gaudet amore tuo.

96.

Calvus, if our sorrow could ever
have any effect on those laid in
the earth, or comfort their silent
dust, then your young wife Quintilia
would be happy and content. But
friends and loves are gone forever
when they have left the light of
the sun. You must be strong my friend
and know that she once loved you.

XCVII.

NON (ita me di ament) quicquam referre putaui,
utrumne os an culum olfacerem Aemilio.
nilo mundius hoc, nihiloque immundius illud,
uerum etiam culus mundior et melior:
nam sine dentibus est. hic dentis sesquipedalis,
gingiuas uero ploxeni habet ueteris,
praeterea rictum qualem diffissus in aestu
meientis mulae cunnus habere solet.
hiç futuit multas et se facit esse uenustum,
et non pistrino traditur atque asino?
quem siqua attingit, non illam posse putemus
aegroti culum lingere carnificis?

97.

I almost can't tell if it makes any difference
greeting Aemilius from the front or behind.
The smell is so awful. Perhaps his ass is less
hideous because it has no teeth. The one he has are a foot long,
his gums are rotting, and his lips are like a donkey's
cunt as it parts on a hot day when she is taking a piss.
He says he fucks the girls. He thinks he's charming.
He is so dumb he can't even walk a miller's donkey
around a grinding wheel. If there's a woman anywhere
who would touch him, she'd have no problem licking the
diseased ass of an aged hangman as he waits between jobs.

XCVIII.

IN te, si in quemquam, dici pote, putide Victi,
id quod uerbosis dicitur et fatuis.
ista cum lingua, si usus ueniat tibi, possis
culos et crepidas lingere carpatinas.
si nos omnino uis omnes perdere, Victi,
hiscas: omnino quod cupis efficies.

98.

Victius, you are the worst of vain and arrogant
scoundrels. Your words are hot air designed to
impress fools. When you open your mouth, the
stench is overpowering. Your tongue is fit only
for licking farmer's boots who've been stomping
in filth all day. No, don't yawn! You will kill us all!

CI.

MVLTAS per gentes et multa per aequora uectus
aduenio has miseras, frater, ad inferias,
ut te postremo donarem munere mortis
et mutam nequiquam alloquerer cinerem.
quandoquidem fortuna mihi tete abstulit ipsum.
heu miser indigne frater adempte mihi,
nunc tamen interea haec, prisco quae more parentum
tradita sunt tristi munere ad inferias,
accipe fraterno multum manantia fletu,
atque in perpetuum, frater, aue atque uale.

101.

I have come across many countries
and across the sea, carrying my
sorrow to your grave, my brother.
My words are too late and fall
unanswered before your silent dust.
I offer you now the ancient gift
rites of the dead wet with my tears.
Hail forever my brother, and farewell.

CIII.

AVT sodes mihi redde decem sestertia, Silo,
deinde esto quamuis saeuus et indomitus:
aut, si te nummi delectant, desine quaeso
leno esse atque idem saeuus et indomitus.

103.

Silo, give me back my ten
sesterces you arrogant prick.
If you want to make money
you should give up being a
pimp, or at least be civil.
In your off hours you can go
back to being a rude punk.

CVIII.

SI, Comini, populi arbitrio tua cana senectus
spurcata impuris moribus intereat,
non equidem dubito quin primum inimica bonorum
lingua exsecta auido sit data uulturio,
effossos oculos uoret atro gutture coruus,
intestina canes, cetera membra lupi.

108.

Cominius, if the people
did themselves a favour
and voted your execution
for your reprehensible crimes,
I would recommend that
they should start by
cutting out your tongue, which is
hostile to the public good,
and throw it to the vultures,
then maybe tear out your eyes
and give them to the crows,
your intestines to the dogs,
and what's left to the wolves.

CXI.

AVFILENA, uiro contentam uiuere solo,
nuptarum laus ex laudibus eximis:
sed cuiuis quamuis potius succumbere par est,
quam matrem fratres efficere ex patruo.

111.

Aufilena, it is a great
honour to live happily in
marriage to a famous Roman;
but when he is your uncle,
the only thing greater is
to be a very skilled whore.

CXII.

MVLTVS homo es, Naso, neque tecum multus homo
te scindat: Naso, multus es et pathicus.

112.

Naso is many men's man though
most men are repulsed by him.
He is always offering pleasure either
bent over or on his hands and knees.

CXIII.

CONSVLE Pompeio primum duo, Cinna, solebant
Maeciliam: facto consule nunc iterum
manserunt duo, sed creuerunt milia in unum
singula. fecundum semen adulterio.

113.

During Pompey's first consulship
Maecilia was handling two men.
During his second consulship
she is still handling two men
but they are different men.
Far down a long list,
adultery as it turns out
has lots of offspring.

GLOSSARY

ARIADNE – A Daughter of Minos the Mythical king of Knosos on the Island of Crete.

BITHYNIA – A roman province in what is now northern turkey.

CALLIMACHUS – A Greek poet and scholar who flourished in Alexandria in the late 3rd century BCE.

CATO – A powerful Roman politician and great grandson of 'Cato the Sensor'.

CHARYBDIS – A monster from whose whirlpool there was no escape.

CICERO (Marcus Tullius) – The greatest roman orator prose writer.

CONSUL – The head civil and military magistrate during the period of the Roman republic.

CYCLEDES – A group of islands in the southern Aegean.

CYRENE – A large Greek city and settlement in north Africa.

HYMENAE – The son of Aphrodite and a god of marriage.

JUPITER AMONS ORACLE – An Egyptian oracle to Jupiter that appeared to have characteristics of both gods.

LESBIA – Catullus's literary name for Claudia Metelli.

MAMURA – A military officer under Caesar who obtained excessive wealth and spent it with great extravagance.

NEMESIS – The goddess of revenge and retrubution.

PARNASSUS – A sacred mountain in central Greece near the site of Delphi.

PELEUS – The mortal husband of the sea nymph Thetis and father of Achilles.

PENELOPE – The wife of Odysseus.

POMPEY – The Roman general who opposed Caesar.

PRAETORS – The title of magistrate chosen to serve as head of state.

RHODES – A large Greek island off the southwest coast of Turkey.

ROMULUS – The mythical founder of Rome.

SALLAI – A ritual associated with Mars.

SCAMANDER – A river in Asia Minor near the ancient site of Troy.

SCYLLA – A six headed monster who ate men alive.

SERAPIS – Greco-Roman variation of an Egyptian cult.

SESTERCE – Roman coin usually made of silver.

TELEMACHUS – The son of Odysseus.

TETHYS – The daughter of Gaia and sister of Ocean.

THESEUS – A legendary king of Athens.

THETIS – A sea-nymph and mother of Achilles.

TRITON – A secondary sea-god.

BIBLIOGRAPHY OF ENGLISH TRANSLATIONS OF CATULLUS

AIEKEN, WILLIAM A., *The Poems of Catullus*, New York: E.P. Dutton & Co., 1950.

ALEXANDER, W. H., *The Book of Catullus of Verona in English Verse*, Edmonton: University of Alberta, 1908.

BURTON, SIR RICHARD FRANCIS and LEONARD C. SMITHERS, *The Carmina of Gaius Valerius Catullus*, London: Printed by the Translators, 1894.

CLUCAS, HUMPHREY, *Versions of Catullus*, London: Agenda Editions, 1985.

CORNISH, FRANCIS WARRE, *The Poems of Gaius Valerius Catullus*, Cambridge: Cambridge University Press, 1904.

CORNISH, F. W., *Catullus*, Cambridge: Harvard University Press, 1913 (revised, G.P. Goold, 1995).

COPLEY, FRANK O., *Complete Poems of Catullus*, Ann Arbor: University of Michigan, 1957.

CRANSTOUN, J., *The Poems of Valerius Catullus*, Edinburgh: W. P. Nimmo, 1867.

DAVIES, JAMES, *Catullus, Tibullus and Propertius*, Edinburgh and London: W. Blackwood & Sons, 1876.

DAVIS, R. K., *Translations from Catullus*, London: G. Bell & Sons, 1913.

DIMENT, RUTH S., *Catullus*, Chicago: Alderbrink Press, 1915.

ELLIS, ROBINSON, *The Poems and Fragments of Catullus*, London: John Murray, 1871.

FLEAY, F. G., *The Poetry of Catullus*, Cambridge: Macmillan & Co., 1864.

FORSYTH, PHYLLIS YOUNG, *The Poems of Catullus*, Lanham: University Press of America, 2002.

GLADSTONE, W.E., *Catullus*, New York: The Modern Library, 1949.

GODWIN, JOHN, *Shorter Poems of Catullus*, London: Aris & Phillips,1999.

GREGORY, HORACE, *The Poems of Catullus*, New York: Grove Press, 1956.

HARRISSON, JOHN A.B., *Selected Poems of Catullus*, Suffolk: Southwold Press, 1980.

DAVIES, THOMAS HART, *Catullus*, Translated into English Verse, London: C. Kegan Paul & Co., 1879.

HILEY, FREDERICK CHARLES WILLIAM, *Selections from Catullus and Horace*, Cambridge: W. Heffer & Sons, 1919.

JAY, PETER, *I Hate and Love, A Selection of Translations from the Poems of C. Valerius Catullus*, London: Outpost Publications, 1963.

KELLY, WALTER K, *Erotica: The poems of Catullus and Tibullus and the Vigil of Venus / A Prose Translation*, London: Henry G. Bohn, 1848.

LAMB, GEORGE, *The Carmina of Catullus*, London: John Murray, 1821.

LEE, GUY, *The Poems of Catullus*, Oxford: Oxford University Press, 1990.

LEVETT, L. R., *Selected Poems of Catullus*, Cambridge: Heffer & Sons, 1905.

LINDSAY, JACK, *The Complete Poetry of Gaius Catullus*, London: Fanfrolico Press, 1929.

MACNAGHTEN, HUGH, *The Poems of Catullus*, Cambridge: Cambridge University Press, 1925.

MARTIN, CHARLES, *Catullus*, Baltimore: Johns Hopkins University Press, 1990.

MARTIN, T., *The Poems of Catullus Translated into English Verse*, London: Parker, Son & Bourn, 1861.

MCLEISH, KENNETH and FREDERICK RAPHAEL, *The Poetry of Catullus*, Boston: D. R. Godine, 1979.

MYERS, RENEY and ROBERT J. ORMSBY, *Catullus*, New York: Dutton, 1970.

MICHIE, JAMES, *The Poems of Catullus*, London: Rupert Hart-Davis Ltd. 1969.

MILLS, BARRISS, *The Carmina of Catullus*, West Lafayette: Purdue University Press, 1965.

NOTT, JOHN, *The Poems of Gaius Valerius Catullus*, London: J. Johnson, 1795.

PACK, RICHARDSON, *Major Pack's Poetical Remains. . . .To which are added, translations from Catullus, Tibullus, and Ovid*, London: E. Curll, 1738.

RABINOWITZ, JACOB, *The Poems of Catullus*, Putnam: Spring Publications, 1991.

SESAR, CARL, *The Selected Poems of Catullus*, New York: Mason & Lipscomb Publisher, 1974.

SISSON, C.H., *The Poetry of Catullus*, New York: Orion Press, 1967.

STUTTAFORD, CHARLES, *The Poems of Gaius Valerius Catullus*, London: G. Bell & Sons, 1912.

SWANSON, ROY ARTHUR, *The Poetry of Catullus*, New York: Liberal Arts Press, 1959.

TREMHEERE, J.H.A., *Poems of Catullus*, New York: Philosophical Library, 1962.

WAY, ARTHUR S., *Catullus and Tibullus in English Verse*, London: Macmillan & Co., 1936.

WHIGHAM, PETER, *The Poetry of Catullus*, London: Penguin, 1966.

WRIGHT, F. A., *Catullus: The Complete Poems*, London: George Routledge & Sons, Limited, 1926.

ZUKOFSKY, CELIA and LOUIS ZUKOFSKY, *Poems of Catullus*, London: Cape Goliard Press, 1969.